Frances Edmonds is a journalist, media personality and dinner speaker, and has been involved in the WellBeing charity cricket matches since their inception in 1989. Her first book, *Another Bloody Tour*, revealed the behind-the-scenes goings-on of the England cricket team abroad, and was an immediate bestseller. She lives in London.

WINNING THE GAME OF LIFE

Tips and Tools for Personal Success

Frances Edmonds

HarperCollins*Publishers*

To my mother Patricia and my daughter Alexandra,
with all my love

HarperCollins*Publishers*
77–85 Fulham Palace Road,
Hammersmith, London W6 8JB

www.**fire**and**water**.com

Published by HarperCollins*Publishers* 2001
1 3 5 7 9 8 6 4 2

A catalogue record for this book
is available from the British Library

ISBN 0 00 257154 4

Set in Utopia
Typeset by Rowland Phototypesetting Ltd,
Bury St Edmunds, Suffolk

Printed and bound in Great Britain by
Omnia Books Limited, Glasgow

contents

acknowledgements   *vii*

preface   *xiii*

CHAPTER ONE   what's your game?   1

CHAPTER TWO   what's your goal?   7

CHAPTER THREE   the goalposts keep changing   17

CHAPTER FOUR   what's your game plan?   25

CHAPTER FIVE   shoot!   37

CHAPTER SIX   sorry, offside!   41

CHAPTER SEVEN   you'll never walk alone   53

CHAPTER EIGHT	your best shot	65
CHAPTER NINE	keep working at it	75
CHAPTER TEN	sick as a parrot, or over the moon?	93
CHAPTER ELEVEN	the art of captaincy	111
CHAPTER TWELVE	leading from the front	129
CHAPTER THIRTEEN	man of the match	145
CHAPTER FOURTEEN	the final whistle	161

acknowledgements

Many people have helped me in this venture and I am enormously indebted to all of them. I am grateful, first and foremost, to Sir Victor Blank, Chairman of Trinity Mirror, Great Universal Stores and also of WellBeing, the charitable arm of the Royal College of Obstetricians and Gynaecologists, and the charity designated to benefit from the net proceeds of this endeavour. Victor is the kind of man who makes things happen and the publication of *Winning the Game of Life* is no exception. I should also like to thank Victor's wife, Sylvia, for her indefatigable hospitality as hostess of the annual WellBeing charity cricket match. In making us all feel so very welcome, both Sylvia and Victor make this event a truly wonderful family occasion. My thanks also to Sir Victor's co-organizer, Sir David Frost, the man whose initial invitation introduced the Edmonds family to the continuing fun and good fellowship of the WellBeing match.

In the formulation of this book, no one could have given more generously of his time, wisdom and experience than Sir Martin Sorrell, Chief Executive Officer of WPP, and 'founder' WellBeing player. His general philosophy of 'Just get on with it!' has been a source of inspiration in my bleaker writer's block/blank screen days and, without the benefit of his 'Nothing is impossible' encouragement, I fear this book might never have been completed. I am also especially grateful to sporting and business entrepreneur Nigel Wray, who devoted much time and thought to this venture and to the issues involved. As the old adage goes, if you want something done, then ask a busy person. Mike Atherton, former England cricket captain, has been another star and his insights, intelligence and wry humour were, and still are, much appreciated. Thanks also to Cliff Morgan, a great friend, a great Welshman and a great rugby international. Cliff is past master of the greatest success secret of them all: how to be loved by everyone all of the time!

Many other WellBeing supporters have gone out of their way to be helpful. They include: Tim Waterstone, Chairman of HMV Media Group plc; David Ross, co-founder of Carphone Warehouse; Archie Norman MP, Chairman of ASDA; John Monks, General Secretary of the TUC; Sir Tim Rice, Oscar award-winning lyricist; Michael Parkinson, writer, broadcaster and Yorkshireman; Sir Anthony Cleaver, Chairman of AEA Technology and the Medical Research Council; Michael Cockerell, award-winning political documentary maker; Sir Derek Robert, The Provost, University College London; Dr Elizabeth Nelson, Chair of the SW London NHS Trust; Dr M. J. Peagram – Deputy Chairman of Yale Catto plc; The Rt Hon. Lord Chadlington, Shandwick plc; Brian Baldock, former Acting-Chairman of Marks & Spencer and Chairman MENCAP; and Mike Brearley, England's most successful cricket captain of all time.

My dear friend Jean, the late Baroness Denton of Wakefield, was as generous as ever in her support of this endeavour. As founder of FORUM UK, an organization which brings together eminent women of diverse achievement, she helped me tap into a rich seam of female experience and perspective. I am grateful to Liz Harman, FORUM's administrator, for her technical and moral support and to the many FORUM members who also gave generously of their time for the benefit of this project. They include: Karen Shepherd, US Executive Director of the European Bank for Reconstruction and Development, former member of the US House of Representatives; Dr Anne Grocock, Executive Director of the Royal Society of Medicine; Sunny Crouch, Managing Director of the World Trade Centre, London; Angela Holdsworth, Lady Neuberger, independent TV producer; Rabbi Julia Neuberger, Chief Executive of The King's Fund; Barbara Hosking, OBE, Deputy Chairman of West Country Television; Julie Baddeley, Executive Director of Woolwich plc; Pamela Langworthy, Director of Thornton's plc; Dame Barbara Mills, DBE, QC, The Adjudicator; Sheila Clark, Managing Director of European Venture Holdings Ltd; Dr Ann Robinson, Director of the General National Association of Pension Funds; Janet Lewis-Jones, Vice-President of the British Board of Film Classification; Ushar Prashar, Chairman of the Parole Board of England and Wales; Diana Ambache, Musical Director of the Ambache Chamber Orchestra; Hilary Sears, VP and Managing Director of the European Consumer Products Practice; AT Kearney Executive Search; Pauline Hyde, President of the Pareregon Group; Janet Ritterman, Director of the Royal College of Music; Dr Liza MacDonald, consultant cancer specialist at Guy's Hospital, London; Sally Field, Associate Fellow, Newnham College, Cambridge; Jaquelin Fisher, Principal of Jaquelin Fisher Associates Environmental Planning; Judith Donovan CBE, Chairman of JDA Direct Mailing; Penelope Rowlatt, Director of Europe Economic Research Ltd; Heather Eggins, Director of the Society for Research into Higher Education; Sue Wilson, Director of the

Inland Revenue, NE Regional Development Agency; Jill Churchill, consultant to BBC Magazines; Gwynneth Flower, Managing Director of Action 2000; Lyndy Payne, Managing Director of the Advertising Agency Register.

My gratitude and untold admiration extends to the hundreds of extraordinary, yet so-called 'ordinary', women involved in Northern Ireland's 'Vital Voices' peace-process conference of spring, 1999. Their thoughts, comments and letters are a constant source of inspiration to me and have proved invaluable in the writing of this book. Through Aideen McGinley, Chief Executive of Fermanagh District Council, I should like to thank you all. There is no one who can teach you anything about vision, determination or the will to win. To Sheila Richards, Rose Fitton and Roberta Brownlee – also many thanks.

Where would we be without a sense of humour? Germany – according to the late and irreplaceable Willie Rushton. Laughter is an absolute must in any long-term undertaking of this nature and for regular injections I should like to thank Tina Knight, Managing Director of Nighthawk Electronics and leading light of the British Association of British Entrepreneurs. For much fun and inspiration, I am also indebted to my good friend, Rachael Heyhoe-Flint, the only English cricket captain never to have lost a test match. For their insights, I am also grateful to Arline Woutersz, President of the British Association of Women Entrepreneurs, to Kirsty Hintz, Chief Executive of Macmaster & Co, and to Keith Benwell of Keith Benwell Associates.

The WellBeing team do a terrific job in ensuring that the welfare of women and their babies is high on the national agenda. No fundraisers could demonstrate more commitment than that displayed by Jane Arnell and her team. For his technical help, my particular thanks to Paul Woodcock. Behind every great man, there is usually a frighteningly efficient personal assistant and Sir Victor Blank's PA is no exception: for all her help, particularly during the initial stages of this book, I am also indebted to the impeccable and unflappable Lora FitzSimons.

Winning the Game of Life was a simple idea which grew and grew and which, in the end, took over two years to complete. I would like to thank my literary agent, Vivienne Schuster at Curtis Brown, for her advice in helping me see this project through. In addition, I am grateful to my publishers at HarperCollins for their belief in, and support of, this WellBeing project. Thanks to former chairman Eddie Bell, to Adrian Bourne, and to all the staff and sales force. In particular, I owe a huge debt of gratitude to my editor, Lucinda McNeile. Whatever her commitments, she was always there with words of support and advice and a clear view of what was necessary. Like all great editors, Lucinda inspires you to feel that, whatever it is you're expected to do, you'll have absolutely no trouble doing it!

Writing is a lonely business and writers need all the friends they can muster. I know I am blessed with a fantastic family, some brilliant mates and the most wonderful daughter. Thank you all for your support and love.

preface

It all began with a cricket match. 1989 saw the creation of one of the country's most enjoyable and successful charity events. Dreamed up by Sir Victor Blank and Sir David Frost, the idea was simple enough, at least for men like Victor and David: eleven international cricketers and eleven captains of industry would engage in a game of cricket, the proceeds of which would go to WellBeing, the charitable arm of the Royal College of Obstetricians and Gynaecologists. The venue was to be the Blank family home in Oxfordshire and the event, although corporately sponsored, was essentially a family affair. Bouncy castles and Bollinger – the amalgam proved irresistible, and the WellBeing cricket match soon became *the* most sought-after invitation in the summer season's social calendar.

The inaugural WellBeing match was imbued with particular significance for me, as it took place just a few weeks after the birth of my own wonderful, happy, healthy daughter, Alexandra. Overwhelmed with gratitude for her safe delivery, I was delighted that my husband Phil, one-time England cricketer, was invited to play in aid of a cause which was at the same time both so worthwhile and so personally meaningful. He went on to enlist the support of the great Australian fast bowler, Dennis Lillee, and the legendary Pakistani all-rounder, Imran Khan. From all sides, cricketing and corporate, the response to the event was tremendous.

The WellBeing cricket match has gone from strength to strength. Over the years, an extraordinary combination of City high flyers, media celebrities and cricketing icons have played with and against one another in a series of highly competitive and hotly contested games. From WPP's Sir Martin Sorrell to New Zealand's Sir Richard Hadlee, from Virgin's Sir Richard Branson to Australia's Shane Warne, and from Burford Holding's Nigel Wray to India's Sunil Gavaskar, the list of individuals, all highly successful in their own spheres, has developed into a *Who's Who* of the business, sporting and media worlds.

And so it was that the original concept of this book was born – a motivational manual to be based on the accumulated knowledge and experience of the WellBeing match's many outstanding supporters. Hundreds of questionnaires, dozens of interviews and far too many lunches later, I found that the original concept had grown out of all recognition. Success, it became clear, comes in many forms, not only those more traditionally acknowledged. From its initial, relatively circumscribed beginnings, the undertaking developed and expanded into far more challenging territory than I had ever anticipated. I have found it, on occasion, a perpendicular learning curve and, at times, a painful exercise in self-discovery and self-assessment. I hope that you will feel, as I do, that *Winning the Game of Life* is worth it.

WINNING THE GAME OF LIFE –
THE WELLBEING PLAN

W ORK – You may be working hard, but are you working effectively?

E NTHUSIASM – Do you feel passionate about what you're doing?

L IFELONG LEARNING – Life is a journey, not a destination. Are you prepared to accept the challenge of lifelong learning as a minimum requirement for the trip?

L EADERSHIP – You may be doing things right, but are you doing the right things and thereby demonstrating key leadership qualities?

B ELIEF – Do you have the courage of your own convictions?

E NERGY – Can you find the energy to keep on trying?

I NSTINCT – Have you the confidence to trust your instincts?

N EVER SAY NEVER – Do you believe that with commitment, determination, hard work and focus you can achieve more than you ever dreamed possible?

G OALS – Are you working towards simple, measurable, achievable, relevant and time-barred goals?

The WellBeing Plan is designed to help you become a key player in the greatest game of all. Start *Winning the Game of Life.*

CHAPTER ONE

what's your game?

It doesn't matter whether you win or lose. It's how you play
the game.

Traditional Saying

Winning the Game of Life is a book for real people living real lives with real
problems. It's a book for people who, like me, struggle to conciliate conflicting demands and who have the honesty to admit that no, we don't always
get it right. It's for people who realize that very few of us can genuinely have
it all. This book will not transform you into Superman or Superwoman.
It won't encourage you to kick ass, flatten competitors or unleash some
hitherto untapped potential which will transform you overnight into Bill
Gates with sex appeal and a sense of humour.

You'll find no pressure within these pages to tap, unleash, grow, expand, or awaken any latent abilities or energies. Neither will you be exhorted to change or perform along any lines other than those you sketch out for yourself. Why add to the mass of performance-related stress already generated by self-help books? No – the message of the book is simply this: Stop beating yourself up! Stop flagellating yourself with the need for constant self-improvement. Whoever you are, you're doing OK so long as you're trying. If you're really trying, then you're already winning the game of life.

This is a book about *you* and *your life*. It's about *feeling* and *being* well. Indeed, this could possibly be a first in international publishing – the first anti-aspirational, motivational book – because this is a book about acceptance. Accept yourself for who and what you are. Give yourself a pat on the back for surviving so far!

You're guaranteed to win the game of life the moment you commit to giving it your very best shot. The game of life has only a few, very simple rules. Better still, you, and only you, are the final arbiter.

GAME OF LIFE RULES

1. Play the game of life with courage and determination, and you are a winner.
2. Play the game of life with honesty and integrity, and you are a winner.
3. Play the game of life with generosity and understanding, and you are a winner.
4. Play the game of life with joy, good humour and good fellowship, and you are a winner.
5. *Believe* that you are winning the game of life and you *are* a winner.

Why do so many people struggle to enjoy the Game of Life? Why do so many turn up to the match armed with the metaphorical sick note from Mum: 'May X be excused? Unfit to play. Not up to it today.' Throw away the sick note and get stuck in! The stadium of life is a no-seater stadium. Spectators are banned from this ground! Winning the game of life means compulsory participation. There is no point hanging around on the sidelines.

Start to take control of the game of life by deciding which game you want to play. Consider your decision carefully or you could end up in the wrong ball game. Don't try competing in the Fame and Fortune League when your unique talents are ideally suited to the Care and Compassion Division. Conversely, don't con yourself into thinking that you'll make the finals of the Mother Teresa of Calcutta Cup when you're odds-on favourite for the Sonofabitch Shield!

Be clear about the game, your position, and how you want to play. In other words, decide who you are, what you want, and where you want to be. When making these decisions, refuse to be sidetracked by other people's ideas and other people's gauges of success. Interesting though these may be, none of them is relevant to the very special, one-off individual which is you. Ignore them! You may find this difficult to begin with and it's hardly surprising. From the earliest days of infancy, we're all subjected to enormous pressure to conform to other people's criteria. From performance on the precocious potty-training stakes to elevation to the peerage, the external yardsticks of achievement insidiously inform our thinking and behaviour. Is it any wonder nowadays that so many people are feeling anxious, stressed-out and frustrated? When an individual's unique talents are neither properly recognized nor remunerated, it's all too easy for him or her to feel rejected, ineffective and worthless. And yet, who's to say that the multimillionaire in the *Sunday Times* Rich List is a more successful human being than the cash-strapped helper giving hope in the hospice? Or that the Nobel Peace Prize winner who can barely remember his children's names is a finer human being than the fantastic foster father?

Success is whatever it is for you. Create your own bespoke definition. Choose your own game. Make your own rules. Ignore the glamorous advertisements on television and in glossy magazines which project images of success based on nothing more substantial than the right car, the right house, the right clothes, the right drink, the right perfume or even (if you want to prove you're a successful mum) the right breakfast cereal or washing powder. ISSIMO lists – league tables of the richest, the most influential, the best-selling, the most coveted – are now a mainstay of Sunday newspaper colour supplements and there's nothing wrong with that. It's all good, clean fun provided that your own personal values aren't unduly influenced or corrupted. Don't allow irrelevant league tables to confuse or deflect you. Let other people play their own conventions. You stick to your own scoring system. Decide for yourself who's winning the game of life. In this game, you're the ref.

Of course, in reaching your own, highly personal decision, you may find it helpful to consider ideas from other people drawn from all walks of life. Some of these may seem completely irrelevant, others may strike a chord. Make a mental note of anything with which you can readily identify and simply ignore the rest.

SO WHO'S A WINNER IN THE GAME OF LIFE?

Do you feel that a winner is someone who manages to find personal satisfaction in his/her own life which, in turn, means leading a balanced existence? Or is it someone who's happy at home with their family, successful in whatever business, job or profession they have chosen, and at the same time, is trying to do something to help the community generally? Is it someone who refuses to measure winning in terms of money, title and power and realizes that, if money is your only yardstick for success, then you'll never be truly satisfied because someone else will always have more than you and therefore you'll always yearn for more?

Maybe you prefer to define a winner as the sort of person you enjoy having around – someone with a positive attitude, who shows initiative and who is fun? Someone who's self-sufficient and has the means to control their own life? Perhaps it's a person who's done things, made things happen in their own field and in their own way, however large or small? Or you may be thinking in terms of an individual who achieves the extraordinary and, at the same time, manages to enjoy an ordinary home life? Someone who sets sensible but challenging personal goals and then consistently overachieves them? Or the person who sets goals and achieves them, but, in the process, motivates others to feel that they are contributing to that achievement?

You may think it's important to lead life in the way you want and, at the same time, to make the most of your abilities and achieve your own expectations (not somebody else's). For you, winning may involve reconciling ambition with personal achievement, or fulfilling your own potential without hurting others and managing to keep your friends. A winner may be someone who has achieved physical, spiritual, mental and emotional wellbeing, or someone who strives for achievement with integrity.

A winner may share broadcaster Michael Parkinson's patented recipe for success: job/hobby; hobby/job – or believe, like Oscar-winning lyricist, Sir Tim Rice, that the only truly successful individual is one who is relaxed, preferably asleep. Perhaps winners are the jugglers who manage to keep most of life's balls in the air.

Is your idea of success a balanced existence, or are you prepared to sacrifice balance in pursuit of success in one specific area? Are personal relationships of paramount importance to you, or are you prepared to sublimate these to the demands of corporate ladder-climbing?

By now, you'll have a clearer picture of the type of success you want to achieve and, by extension, the kind of individual you want to be. Whatever your vision of a winner, be honest about it. It doesn't matter whether you aspire to be the best barmaid in the Bull and Bush in Bolton or the biggest bastard billionaire in Bermuda. This is *your* definition. Think carefully before you make your decision, because it's going to dictate your game plan.

CHAPTER TWO

what's your goal?

The world stands aside for a man who knows where he is going.

Earl Nightingale

A bad ending follows a bad beginning.   Euripides

We all have dreams but, for the sake of argument, let's try visualizing the ultimate dream of every soccer player in the world. Imagine yourself, tears streaming down your cheeks (you are, after all, a footballer), as you hold the Jules Rimet World Cup aloft to the cheers of an ecstatic crowd. The vision could not be more clear or more potent. Inspired, you now feel you want to go ahead and make that dream a reality. You know what you want to achieve and, once that six-pack in the fridge is finished, you're going to apply yourself to achieving it.

The sad fact is, however, that you are fifty-five, three stone overweight and the proud possessor of two left feet. The closest you'll ever get to sporting glory is a collection of acrylic replica shirts and a malodorous pair of Nike trainers. Don't worry – there's nothing to be ashamed of. You're one of the 99 per cent of British blokes who, despite the balding pate and beer belly, believes he's a cross between David Beckham and Pierce Brosnan. Dreaming never hurt anyone but, without realistic goals, no dream can become a reality. You must be honest and objective about what you can achieve. This doesn't mean you shouldn't push your abilities and talents to the limit, but if you overestimate your capabilities you may be doomed to constant frustration.

SET YOURSELF CLEARLY DEFINED GOALS

Set yourself clearly defined, realistic goals. These goals may not be easy to achieve ('I want to achieve financial security for the rest of my life' or 'I want to be physically fit'), but at least they are easy to comprehend.

> Be clear about what you want to achieve: it's easier to hit a clear target than a blurred one.

Think of a journey: if you don't have a clear idea of your destination before you set out, how can you be sure that you're travelling in the right direction? The same holds true for the game of life: if you don't have a clear idea of what you want to achieve in life, how can you even set about achieving it?

> Those who do not set goals are doomed forever to work for those who do.
>
> *Brian Tracy*

Without clearly defined goals, you can't measure whether you're winning or losing. How can you know that you're making progress in the journey of your own life? To track your own development, you need to set yourself targets. Your goals must be focussed and specific. An elite athlete might well decide 'I want to win the gold in the men's one hundred metres at the next Olympic Games.' The owner of a business might determine 'to increase profits by 10 per cent over the next financial year'. A GCSE student might aim for ten A grades in his or her forthcoming examinations. Your goals, however, may be vague and ill-defined: 'I'd like to be better at running', 'I'd like to make more money', or 'I'd like to do well in my exams.' They may be ambitious: 'I want to be prime minister by the age of forty-five.' Or they may seem relatively banal: 'I want to spring-clean the house this week.' It doesn't matter how trite or trivial your goals may seem to other people, it's still important for you to set them, whatever they may be. But the more specific the goal, the more focussed your efforts. And the more focussed your efforts, the greater your chance of achieving positive results.

DECIDE WHAT YOU REALLY WANT . . .

Give yourself some quiet time to reflect and to plan what you really want.

Far too many people lead lives so frenetic that they never seem to have the time to stop and consider what they really want. Remember, without a clear end in mind, it's impossible to travel in the right direction.

. . . AND KEEP IT SIMPLE

Never allow the power of your overall vision to become lost in excessive detail. Adopt broad brush strokes. Paint a clear picture of your destination, sketch in the major landmarks along the way, but allow yourself the freedom of deciding how best to get there.

> If the destination is truly attractive, you'll always find the map.

Pursue Projects You Passionately Believe in

We all know how easy it is to pursue something we love doing, or something we believe in passionately. When you're doing the things you love, time stands still and the hours fly by unnoticed. Try to involve yourself in pursuits in which you're genuinely interested. Time spent feeling fully involved is invariably time best spent.

Set Yourself SMART Goals

In deciding on your own personal mission statement, don't fall into the trap of getting carried away. Stick to SMART goals: simple, measurable, achievable, relevant and time-barred. As we've already seen, a clear, simple objective, such as scaling Mount Everest, may be anything but simple to achieve. The highest mountains, both actual and metaphorical, are conquered by adopting a step-by-step approach. In other words, when confronted with a major challenge, set yourself a series of simple, short-term goals and focus on achieving them.

The prospect of writing an eighty-thousand-word book may seem overwhelming, but the prospect of writing one thousand words a day for eighty days is far easier to contemplate. Once you realize that you can achieve your simple, bite-sized goals, your confidence will grow and you'll find it easier to set new, reasonable, manageable and, perhaps, even more challenging objectives.

Don't be frightened of failure, and don't start beating yourself up if the goals you set are not always achieved. Whatever the outcome, you'll have learned something along the way. Failure does not equal disgrace. Even the most highly successful and motivated people have experienced some degree of failure in their lives. In fact, game of life winners probably experience more setbacks than others because they are not afraid to take up new and more difficult challenges. The great ice hockey player, Wayne Gretzky, once observed that 'You miss 100 per cent of shots that you never take', and we all know that the man who never made a mistake never made anything. Winners make mistakes, lots of them. The difference between winners and losers, however, is that winners *learn* from their mistakes. They refuse to be floored by failure. They put their setbacks down to experience, draw the relevant conclusions, then move on to the next challenge.

The exercise of fixing objectives is enormously powerful. It creates a positive dynamic which helps us move forward in our lives. Each goal we reach inspires us with more confidence. Start by setting short-term, manageable goals and you'll notice how swiftly 'many a little makes a mickle'. Don't allow yourself to be daunted by the apparent enormity of your aspirations. Remember, even the longest journey starts with one small step.

Simple Goals

If you want to be able to monitor your own personal progress easily, you must keep your goals clear and well-defined. 'I want to lose weight' may be a laudable objective, but it's far too sloppy and nebulous. Consider, by contrast, the following statement: 'I resolve to lose two pounds per week until I've lost fourteen pounds.' Now you're talking! Now you really *are* on the way to shedding that unwanted fat. Why? Because you're *planning* your weight-loss campaign, not merely *talking* about it. And if you want to be even *more* effective, adopt a still more positive approach: focus on what you want to be or become as opposed to what you no longer want to remain. Compare 'I want to lose weight' with the following statement: 'I want to be slim, to feel better in my clothes and to have more vitality and energy. In order to achieve all these goals, my ideal target weight is X. And in order to achieve this target weight, I must lose two pounds per week for Y weeks.' The first statement is limp and vague, while the second is positive, precise and easy to monitor.

In exactly the same way, statements such as 'I hate my job/this relationship/this situation' are pointless unless accompanied by a resolution to change things for the better by first deciding what you *do* want, e.g., 'I want to be self-employed. I want a happy, supportive relationship or none at all. I want to feel secure and in control of my life.' Whatever the target, once it's been set you can start measuring your progress towards it.

Measurable Goals

Nothing is more depressing or demotivating than the uphill struggle to meet unrealistic targets. Goals may be demanding, perhaps even gruelling, but they should never be utterly impossible. We're all familiar with the 'Crash Diet' syndrome – slimming based on near-starvation regimes where those dieting lose twenty pounds in one month only to regain all the lost pounds (and more!) once the *unrealistic and unsustainable* target has been reached. No one can learn to run a marathon in half an hour. The training process is one of gradual progression as stamina and pain control are systematically and incrementally increased. With the exception of lottery winners and IT whizz kids, few people make millions overnight. The vast majority of success stories involve hard work and sacrifice in pursuit of the ultimate objective.

Achievable Goals

Focussing on achievable targets does not mean going for the easy option. Be brave! Never allow yourself to compromise for fear of failure. Once you've fixed on an objective and decided on a course of action (strategy and tactics), remove all thoughts of negative consequences from your mind. The surest way to miss a penalty shot is to start thinking you might not get it. The surest way to score a goal is to visualize that ball already in the back of the net. Be positive and proactive. Don't sit back passively and expect everything in life to turn up trumps. It won't. You'll simply end up finding that you're being swept along with the tide. Don't be frightened to grasp opportunities just because you're worried about what other people might say if you fall flat on your face. Worrying about other people's opinions is the best recipe for paralysis and failure. Manchester United star, David Beckham, has his fair share of detractors. But how many goals would he score if, every time he went out on to the pitch, he started to think about the cruel jibes and negative comments to which he is constantly subjected in the media? Learn to ignore other people. Concentrate on *your* game. Focus on *your* agenda. This is, after all, the game of *your* life.

> Win by consistently meeting your short-term,
> achievable targets.

Relevant Goals

Everyone, even the most focussed individuals, will encounter occasional distractions while pursuing their aims. When there is continued dislocation between real aims or goals and everyday behaviour, however, the result is usually unease and confusion. It is therefore essential that we clarify our real aims by focussing on a set of values specific and relevant to us. As we are all individuals with different talents, backgrounds, principles and energy levels, no two people will have precisely the same goal. Your goal may involve a grandiose plan to float your company on the Stock Exchange or it may be the deceptively simple aspiration to understand yourself better. Your own personal goal or set of goals will form the basis of your own personal mission statement.

> Living life in a way which is consistent with your own individual set of values is the only way to ensure your own general wellbeing and personal satisfaction.

Draw up a list of personal and professional goals. To make this easier, consider what gives you most satisfaction. Do you yearn to be proved right over time and create something worthwhile for posterity? Or perhaps you'd rather be considered the best at what you do by clients and competitors alike? Maybe you'd like to work with excellent, inspirational people, enjoy their respect, build teams and watch other people around you succeed and develop their potential. Ethical or environmental considerations may play a significant part in your overall game plan. Satisfaction for Sir Tim Rice is simply 'handing something in'; for Michael Parkinson it's 'laughing at something I've written'; for former England cricket captain, Mike Atherton, it's 'scoring tough runs, that's to say runs against top bowlers in difficult circumstances'. In other words, it doesn't matter how grand or how humble your objective is as long as it's relevant to *you*.

Goals, whether personal or professional, must be relevant and to be relevant, they must be rooted in values, vision and priorities which are *yours*. Decide what is at your core. Understand what makes you tick. What is your major organizing principle? Is it your husband or your wife? Children or friends? Work? Money? Possessions? Religion, sport or politics? Control or influence? Recognition or fame? Be honest! We can all spot the Miss World 'I'd like to help others and save the planet' routine at a thousand paces. When the goals you set are truly consistent with your own values, you're far more likely to find the commitment necessary to achieve them.

> Keep your goals relevant to you.

Time-Barred Goals

Everyone needs the discipline of deadlines. Without deadlines, it's difficult to generate the sense of urgency that achievement and progress demand. Without deadlines, the mañana philosophy kicks in. For goals to be effective, they must be time-barred. Some people find that making lists of daily, weekly, monthly and annual goals is a good way of monitoring their own personal and professional development. Other people prefer to determine goals in different areas of their lives (family/work/social) and then allot a specific timespan to each of these goals. Whichever way you decide to go about it, it's essential to set specific targets and observe how well they have been met within a given length of time. The act of time-barring your goals facilitates both monitoring and momentum.

The discipline of planning is useful, but don't let your planning become so rigid that it precludes spontaneity. We all need some leeway if we're going to be able to grasp unforeseen opportunities when they arise. Neither should you schedule your goals so punctiliously ('By my twenty-fifth birthday, I want to be a doctor/lawyer/happily married mother of three') that you feel a total failure if you are unable to adhere precisely to your pre-ordained timetable. Goal-setting is essential to activate change, and deadlines are equally essential in maintaining momentum. But don't be too hard on yourself if you can't always make or do things on time. The very fact of time-barring adds impetus to your efforts. For that reason alone, it's a useful exercise to adopt.

CHAPTER THREE

the goalposts keep changing

If there is one thing in life that is certain, it is that nothing in life is certain.

Traditional

Look around you and you can't help noticing that the world about you is in a state of permanent revolution, constantly adapting to social, economic and technological changes. Everyone feels comfortable with the familiar, with the status quo. We all feel uneasy contemplating the unknown factors involved in change. But if we want not only to survive but also to thrive in this rapidly developing universe of ours, we must face both the inevitability and the challenge of change.

Charles Darwin famously observed that the creatures who adapt most easily and readily to change have the greatest chance of surviving and evolving successfully. As human beings, we're at a distant advantage over most other creatures in the animal kingdom: we possess the intellectual wherewithal to effect *internal* or *personal* change. Whatever the change, we must learn how to plan in order to direct that change to a successful conclusion.

The key to managing change lies in careful, well crafted planning.

More often than not, external change is beyond our control: it occurs whether we welcome it or not. Every one of you can probably think of some unwelcome external change that's had a profound effect on your life. Perhaps a parent or a loved one has died. Perhaps a relationship has broken up. Maybe you've borne the brunt of economic circumstances beyond your control which lead to you losing your job. Perhaps, through no fault of your own, you've been involved in an accident which has left you unable to work or even permanently disabled. It may even be that greater penetration of information technology and an increase in Internet usage has meant that you've been forced to radically re-think the way you conduct your business.

All these are instances of external changes over which you have absolutely no control, but which nonetheless demand a response and, implicit in that response, a *change* from you.

On a personal level, there are internal changes that *you* decide *you* must make in order to deal with life as you are experiencing it. Imagine, for example, that you find yourself confronted with the unwelcome, external change of redundancy. You may elect to make the internal change of acquiring new skills in order to secure a new job. At an even more traumatic level, imagine you were to be disabled by the external tragedy of a serious accident. You would then be confronted with the daunting challenge of making the internal physical and psychological changes necessary to cope with life in a wheelchair. Change cannot simply be ignored; change demands some sort of reaction. Winners in the Game of Life will choose a positive response.

> It's not what happens to you that matters, it's how
> you choose to deal with it.

These are examples of *external* changes which demand an *internal* response. Other changes we decide to make are not so obviously linked to an *external* stimulus, but are suggested to us from within. We may never have experienced the need for radical change that cancer, a heart attack, a business disaster or an unexpected divorce precipitates. We may be moved by the need for change simply because we do not feel healthy enough, secure enough, happy enough, useful enough, skilled enough . . . It could well be the case that no obvious *external* factors are forcing us to change, but rather a deeper need *within*. Our aspirations for constant improvement demand that we keep on making changes.

> Education is the ability to meet life's
> constant changes.

It doesn't matter whether the changes you need to make to keep winning the game of life are externally or internally driven. The fundamental question remains the same: how are you going to handle them? How can you motivate yourself to make *internal* changes? And when you find yourself confronted by *external* change, are you prepared to make the effort to manage that change proactively, or are you just going to sit back and allow change to dictate to you and to control you? To be a winner in the game of life, there's really no choice in the matter. You know that if you don't take charge of change, then change, by default, takes charge of you.

> Fail to plan and you plan to fail.

In order to manage change of any kind, you've got to work out a game plan. If you don't have a game plan, you'll find yourself wasting both time and energy. In other words, you'll find yourself wasting your life. The only advantage in refusing to plan is that failure will come as a complete surprise without the preceding stress or worry. But fail you will. Every game needs a game plan. To win the game of *your* life, you'll need to think carefully about the kind of game you want to play and the kind of life you want to lead.

Very few of us find life's constant changes easy to handle. Most of us view change as downright unwelcome, even though the ultimate consequences of that change may be extremely positive. A woman I interviewed runs an extremely successful software company. A few years before she went into business, she was diagnosed with breast cancer which eventually resulted in a double mastectomy. It was at this point that her husband of fifteen years decided to run off with his secretary, leaving her with two children and no job. Her life, prospects, expectations and self-image suddenly collapsed around her. She became depressed, could barely find the energy to drag herself out of bed in the morning in order to take her children to school and then spent most of the day in tears.

Then something happened which brought her to with a start. Distractedly driving her children home from school one afternoon, she narrowly missed a woman wheeling a pram across a zebra crossing. 'It was in that split second of panic,' she recalls, 'that I realized things had got to change. In fact, more specifically, I knew that *I* had to change.'

So what did she do? First, she stopped *reacting* like a victim, and started behaving more proactively. She enlisted the help of a family-law solicitor, who left her errant husband in no doubt as to his moral, legal and financial responsibilities towards herself and their two children. The mere fact of *doing* something increased her self-confidence. Second, having achieved some degree of financial security for herself and her family, she began to think positively about what she could do with the rest of her life. She drew up a list of all her attributes (personable, able to drive, willing to work hard) and soon landed herself a job as a saleswoman with an up-and-coming software company. Within six months she had doubled the company's turnover and within a year was offered a partnership.

Ten years later, that same woman is running a successful business, looks a million dollars, and is worth rather more. She has brought up two children of whom she can be justifiably proud and has recently married a man she met while she was trekking in India. She is a firm believer that God helps those who help themselves. 'And the best way to help yourself', she observes, 'is to sit down and work out a plan.'

PROACTIVE PLANNING IS MORE POWERFUL THAN PROZAC

We all have areas of our lives where we've either been obliged to change or where we now desperately want to change or improve. Think of all the things which you're constantly meaning to change and which, somehow, you've never got around to dealing with. You may want to lose weight, quit smoking, reduce the amount of alcohol you drink, or exercise more regularly. You may want to do things you haven't even tried yet: change jobs, write a book, learn a new language or finally get to grips with that computer which has been lying around untouched since it was removed from the box! Or you may even want to try things you've never had the courage to try: activities such as scuba-diving, public speaking, acting or singing.

If you're honest with yourself, you'll probably find scores of things you'd like to do or to change. So what's stopping you from doing any or all of those things you *think* or *talk* about doing? Don't hide behind the raft of excuses we call 'other people'. The only real obstacle that lies between us and untold opportunities for our growth is our own fear of change: we're frightened of the unknown.

Even the most ostensibly confident people are frightened of something. One woman I interviewed recalls sharing a platform with a well-known and outspoken politician on BBC television's *Question Time*. When she glanced down at the hands of this hard-hitting, aggressive political Rottweiler, she was amazed to see that they were shaking, and they continued to shake throughout the entire programme. And yet, from his performance, no one would ever have guessed he was nervous.

> Winners in the game of life are also nervous and frightened, but they learn to sublimate their fear and to get on with things regardless.

Whatever your bogeyman – public speaking, driving in the dark, flying, climbing up a ladder – no one is exempt from fear. Many of us know brilliant and competent people who could knock the socks off the people around them if only they could assert themselves. We've all met individuals who'd rather die than make a decision. They seem to spend their lives in agonies of prevarication. Some people are frightened of intimacy ('I can't get involved with this person. What if he or she lets me down/betrays me/runs off with someone else?'); of changing jobs ('I really hate what I'm doing, but at least I know the ropes here'); of being alone ('I can't abide my husband/wife/ partner but it's better to have someone than to risk being alone'); of growing old; of losing a loved one; of ending a relationship that's going nowhere; or even of something as simple as swimming!

Whatever it is, we've all got something we're frightened of, something we think we can't do. Game of life winners are not immune to fears and doubts, but they know how to turn 'CAN'T DO' into 'CAN DO' by creating a game plan to win.

It all sounds so simple. Figure out a plan for winning the game of your life and implement it. Why is it that the question 'Do you have a plan for your life?' meets with such resistance? Can you feel yourself backing off already? Are you saying to yourself that you can't really plan your life? Or that you're not really sure what you want to do? Or that there's no point in planning because you can't do what you *really* want to do and, in any event, planning only leads to disappointments?

It may be that you do have a very definite plan for your career, but that there's nothing in place for all the other areas of your life. And yet how can you know if you're winning in your life if you don't have a plan against which to measure all your achievements? If you really want to win the game of *your* life, take time out to create your own individual game plan.

CHAPTER FOUR

what's your game plan?

It's not the will to win that counts. Everybody has that. It is the will to *prepare* to win that counts.

Bear Bryant

You're planning to win the game of *your* life, so it's important to create a game plan that's tailored to meet your specific needs and requirements. To be successful, your individual game plan must take into account all aspects of you and your life: physical, mental, emotional and spiritual. At the same time, your game plan must ensure that what you're doing now, and in the short term, is of help to you in reaching your long-term objectives. And finally, before you start to implement your game plan – before you even kick off – be clear about your ultimate goals: know what you want to achieve.

THE GAME OF LIFE GAME PLAN

What Kind of Player Am I?

Warm up by asking yourself what kind of a person you really are, and what core beliefs you espouse. Perhaps you have strongly held religious beliefs which will influence your game plan, or you may share more general moral beliefs such as the 'Do as you would be done by' ethic. Perhaps you passionately believe that people are more important than politics, that the customer is always right, that no person should be discriminated against on the basis of gender, colour, sexual preference or creed. Take time to consider your fundamental beliefs and values as these will have a fundamental bearing on the game plan that's right for you.

Which Titles Am I After?

Don't be afraid to be honest. Whatever you say, no one else has the right to sit in judgement on you. Do you truly value other people, building personal relationships and communicating with others? Or do you in fact think that diamonds are a girl's best friend? Perhaps, after years on the treadmill of a demanding career, you've decided to place greater value on relaxation. If so, you could consider how you'd like to use that leisure time more effectively – would you like to invest in your personal development by reading, attending evening classes, taking courses or acquiring a new skill? Perhaps you'd like to have more time to see your friends or to stay at home with your family. Do you want to travel, meet new people and experience different cultures? Or perhaps, like one friend of mine, you'd like to take up a physical challenge such as learning to ride a motorbike? (The friend in question is fifty-five and the glamorous granny of three!) Decide what's genuinely important to you. This also will affect your game plan.

Who you are now and what you want to be and do will all be conditioned by your environment and by life as you've experienced it so far. In working out your future game plan, think about where you're coming from.

What's My Track Record?

Your experience of life thus far will have a significant bearing on why you *feel* and *act* the way you do now. Some of the influences in your life will be positive. If, for example, you were lucky enough to have been brought up surrounded by creative people full of flair and imagination, there's every chance that some of that creative genius will have rubbed off on you. Perhaps, without even realizing it, you've internalized your parents' characteristics of honesty, integrity and hard work, which explains your current status as a pillar of the local community. On the other hand, you may have reacted against these very characteristics and are currently robbing banks!

Everyone can think of influences that have impacted negatively on their lives. Perhaps you had parents who constantly denigrated your achievements and made you feel that nothing you ever did was good enough. Perhaps you have a partner who's forever nagging you to keep up with the Joneses? Many people find their self-confidence and self-esteem flattened by such pernicious influences. Others react by exhibiting indefatigable drive which results in constant overachievement. Only when we understand the influences at work on us, can we understand and, if we so desire, change our reactions to them. A track record is just that. A record of *past* performance.

With a well thought-out plan, you can raise your game. You can decide on *future* performance.

Where Do I Really Score?

How often do you consider all the skills and abilities you've acquired over the years? The chances are it's only when you're compiling your CV or applying for a job. So here's a golden opportunity to be generous with yourself. Hype yourself up a bit. None of this 'I'm *only* a housewife' routine. Just hang on a minute! Think about the range of jobs the average housewife does. As home manager, she balances a budget, deals with interpersonal issues, resolves conflicts, acts as a trainer, educator, entertainments officer, resident logistics expert, psychotherapist, counsellor, restaurateur and hotelier. The average housewife is, in computer terminology, a multiplexor par excellence, capable of performing numerous different functions at the same time. In other words, there's no such thing as *only a housewife*. No one is *only* anything. Each and every one of us is a rich and complex mixture of talents and abilities.

Be sure not to minimize your skill set. Think about *all* the things you can do and are capable of doing. Find the time to write them all down. You'll be surprised how impressive you are!

Up Front, at the Back or Midfield?

In formulating your game plan, it's important to understand your own personality and temperament. If you think it might be useful, enlist the support of a close friend to help you consider the question. After all, if you're not clear about your own personality, you'll run the risk of making the wrong personal and professional decisions. If you recognize that you're the shy, sensitive, retiring type, you'll probably realize that a career in sales would be a mistake. And if you're like Patsy in *Absolutely Fabulous*, then it's probably best not to pursue a high-flying career in the Foreign and Commonwealth Office.

Once you've answered these questions honestly and exhaustively, you'll have a clearer picture of yourself and a clearer idea of your game plan. Many people who feel unhappy and frustrated are stuck in a rut because they've never taken the time to understand who they truly are or what they really want. They've set off in what they thought was the right direction only to find out later that they were using the wrong map.

For twelve years I worked as an international conference interpreter for all the major international organizations. For about six of those years I was happy, busily concocting linguistic silk purses out of other people's syntactic sows' ears. I enjoyed the freedom of travelling to conferences all over the world. I loved the good fellowship and fun of my highly intelligent colleagues. I relished the stimulation of getting to grips with complicated issues in various different languages. And I liked the financial independence conferred by doing the job.

After about seven years, however, I could feel I was going stale. The learning curve had levelled out, the idea of travel was no longer so exciting and, even worse, I was no longer interested in listening to whatever the politicians had to say. Not only was I not interested in *listening* to what they said, but, more worrying still, certainly I was not interested in *translating* it!

It's difficult to cope with a midlife crisis when you're still in your twenties! What was I supposed to do? Throw away a massive investment of time and education? After all, I'd spent three years at Cambridge, reading modern languages, and had devoted large chunks of my life to studying in

France, Italy and Spain. I'd been trained as an interpreter by the best linguists in Europe. Furthermore, not only was interpreting my profession, but it had become the main organizing principle in my social life: the peripatetic nature of the job meant that most of my friends were associated with the profession.

I knew I had to change, but it took over two years to understand what I really wanted to do (write) and another three to muster the guts to give up a comfortable, relatively secure and eminently sociable existence for the vagaries of self-employment and the solitude of scribbling. Change, however necessary, is rarely easy. The alternative, however, is worse: the risk of frustration, unhappiness and boredom – it's death by a thousand cuts.

Once you've established who and what you are *now*, it's time to move on to the next stage of the plan: how to become who and what you want to be in the *future*.

What Kind of Player Do I Want to Be?

Begin by asking yourself the fundamental question: what is it in my life that gives me most satisfaction? Again, it's worth taking some time over this issue. How many people do you know who achieve their desired goals and reach their projected destination only to realize that their success has left them neither happy, fulfilled nor satisfied? Take the classic example of the man who works all hours to build his fortune and then realizes, to his horror, that he's become a virtual stranger to his wife and children. Or the astronaut who returns to earth and finds that life after space is a depressing anticlimax. As the old adage runs: Be careful what you pray for. The chances are you'll get it.

Once you've drawn up a list of the things which give you most satisfaction (family, friends, work, helping other people succeed, making money, being proved right, etc.), it's time to ask yourself *why* you find those things so satisfying. It may be feelings of warmth, empathy and love that genuine friendship engenders. It may be the buzz of power and influence that a high-powered City job confers. Perhaps your satisfaction comes from the security of money, the thrill of watching your children develop, or simply the joy of watching your garden bloom in spring.

What's Given Me the Biggest Buzz?

Try to think of the most fulfilling moment in your life or career to date. This may be anything from giving birth to a child or singing in the chorus in the local amateur dramatic society, to setting up your own company and becoming a market leader.

Ask yourself *why* this particular achievement gave you such a buzz? Precisely *how* did you feel when you reached it?

What Motivates Me, and Why?

Are you motivated by the fact that you passionately enjoy doing what you're doing? Is it because you're having fun? Are you motivated by a need to prove yourself, or by your feelings of responsibility to provide for yourself and your family?

Am I Happy Playing in My Current Position?

Don't be afraid of saying no, even though no implies that you should be making changes you may not feel ready or strong enough to make.

Can I Continue to Improve in My Current Position?

Does your current career or lifestyle provide you with opportunities to develop? If so, what are they? These may be opportunities to train, acquire additional skills, travel, meet new people, assume increased responsibility, learn how to work as part of a team or how to be a team leader. Do you find these potential opportunities an exciting proposition?

Am I Happy to be Just a Journeyman Player?

If future growth opportunities are not present in your current career or life, does this bother you? If the answer is no, then you're obviously not feeling disappointed or frustrated *enough* to start ringing the changes. If, however, your answer is affirmative, it's time to take control by creating your game of life plan.

By now you should have a clearer picture of who and what you'd like to be. Don't worry if your aspirations seem overambitious. However hard you try, you may never succeed in looking like Linda Evangelista, singing like Kiri Te Kanawa or playing tennis like André Agassi, but don't lose heart. Remember, you're playing the game of *your* life and, although you may never be the *absolute* best in any area of endeavour, you can certainly achieve fulfilment by achieving a personal best.

What Kind of Player Can I Be?

Ask yourself what would be your ideal lifestyle. Most children have the gift of untrammelled imagination. When we're small, we all have dreams of our ideal career and lifestyle and we're convinced that we can be whatever we want to be. As time goes by, however, and we take a few of life's hard knocks, reality and compromise begin to kick in. Try to reel back to your childhood. Allow your imagination free rein. Accept no restrictions. Remember what you desperately wanted to be and do.

What's Holding You Back?

Consider what's precluding or inhibiting you from pursuing your ideal lifestyle. It may be common sense. Let's face it, at seventy-five, you're just too old to start your bid for the Tour de France. You may dream of sailing single-handedly around the world but realize that the demands of your three small children will preclude your trying it. But dreams need not be so grandiose. Perhaps you only want a job in the local department store but feel that your shape, size or sex is against you. You may simply want more peace, quiet and time to yourself, but find that this is impossible in a hectic family environment. List all the obstacles which are standing between you and the life you want to lead.

When Do I Back Off?

You may have to make certain compromises in your current personal or professional life in order to be able to pursue your ideal lifestyle. Every action has an equal and opposite reaction. Change in one area of your life will inevitably precipitate change in other areas. If, for example, you seriously want to improve your job prospects by acquiring new skills at night school, then those regular soirées in the wine bar will just have to go. And if you're absolutely determined to get fit, then the forty-cigarettes-a-day routine will have to disappear.

Before you start making any changes, however, consider the impact of your decision to change on the people around you. In most cases, you'll need the understanding and support of others to help you see the changes through. You may feel, after due discussion, that your game plan is over-ambitious or fails to take into account the legitimate needs of the key stake-holders around you. If so, ask yourself which compromises can and cannot be made in order to ensure fair play for everyone.

Can I Find a Better Sweat-To-Bread Ratio?

After careful thought, you may discover that the sort of life or growth potential you seek can be achieved with less hassle.

Let's take the example of a friend of mine, a middle-aged woman who cares deeply about people and who yearned to retrain and become a doctor. My friend knew that the minimum of six years study required to realize this dream would place an excessive strain on her husband, three children and the family finances. Her dream to become a doctor was unrealistic at that

time, but she refused to throw in the towel. She realized that her fundamental desire was to help and care for other people and that this could be
channelled into other branches of the caring professions. In the end, she
selected a course in counselling and is currently working on an occasional
basis for the Samaritans. She has fulfilled her need to help others without
disrupting her own domestic arrangements.

Where's the Coach?

As Otto von Bismarck once said, 'Only a fool learns from his own experience.
A wise man learns from the experience of others.'

While you're planning and trying to make changes in your life, you may
find it useful to refer to a mentor, someone whom you can trust, who under-
stands your issues, and who has been through your projected mill himself.
For personal problems, you may choose to confide in a member of your
family, a friend or a professional counsellor. For more work-related concerns, you may prefer to discuss matters with a colleague or a careers
adviser. Whatever the problem, never be afraid to ask for advice. Most
people are usually flattered to be asked and only too happy to lend their
support.

Work-related issues are often less difficult to deal with than personal
problems. In contemplating a job or a career, you must be clear what you
want from it. For some people, salary will be the most important issue. For
others, perhaps those with children, the idea of flexible working hours is far
more significant than salary alone. You may want a job which stretches you,
which pushes you beyond your usual comfort zone and demands that you
improve your skills and release your hitherto untapped potential. Ask yourself whether you want the autonomy of working alone, or whether you

prefer the banter and camaraderie of working in a team. Is the job security of a staff position crucial to your mental wellbeing, or are you prepared to accept the insecurities that go hand-in-hand with the freedom of a self-employed existence? Are you highly self-motivated, or would you stay in bed all day, watching television, if you didn't have the imposed discipline of an external timetable to guide you? Perhaps you want to work for a company where there's scope for worldwide travel and rapid promotion, or maybe you'd prefer a company whose expectations fit in more readily with your complicated domestic arrangements? What do *you* require to make you feel happy in your work? What gives you most job satisfaction?

Personal change is usually more difficult to cope with because the impetus must *always* come from within. There are, however, any number of support groups covering every issue from weight loss to alcohol abuse. Don't be afraid or embarrassed to seek the support of others in creating the game plan you need to win the game of life.

CHAPTER FIVE

shoot!

Success is not so much a question of optimism or pessimism.
The fact is that decisive people are winners, and ditherers
are losers.

Cliff Morgan, Welsh Rugby International

The time must come when all the planning, thinking, consulting and deliberating must stop and you've simply got to get on with playing the game of life.

Stop hanging around, making Hamlet look like
Indiana Jones. Just do it!

Planning is one thing, mustering the guts to take the plunge is quite another. We're all afraid of the unknown, but the risks involved in going into the unknown decrease with experience and information. It may sound contradictory, but before you just do it, make sure you've done as much preparation on your game plan as possible. Think of all the angles. Analyse all the permutations. Rehearse the possible upsides and downsides. After all, no one walks the tightrope without a few preliminary excursions using a safety net.

Before taking the plunge, you must believe with your heart and soul that you *can* do whatever it is you're setting out to achieve. There is, of course, a slight catch-22 element in all this. Doing something successfully will give you more self-belief and self-confidence. This is true of every pursuit, from sex to scuba-diving. Don't be too anxious to kick off. Pretend you're feeling confident. With practice, the real thing will arrive.

FAKE IT TILL YOU MAKE IT!

So there you are, up there on the dais about to address the convention, on the springboard about to dive, on the brink of remortgaging your home in order to set up the new business you've always dreamed of running, or on the verge of signing the legal papers that will end a marriage that's been draining you for years. This is the danger zone where fear of the unknown may trigger hesitation. In these situations, there's only one solution: stop thinking! If you've planned carefully, done the groundwork and thought it all through, now is the time for action. Now is the time to allow your subconscious to take over and fill your thoughts with positive, get-on-with-it messages: 'He who hesitates is lost', 'The more I practise, the luckier I get', 'Once more unto the breach, dear friends, once more' – whatever they are, find some form of words or mental stimulus that moves you along. Once you have that 'stop-messing' message embedded in your subconscious, you can call it up at any time to help vault you over the immediate hurdle into positive 'Can Do – Have Done' territory.

What next? After the event, ask yourself which was worse: the anticipation of the event or the event itself? Generally speaking, you'll find the *doing* is far less alarming and far less exhausting than the *contemplation of the doing*. The same principle applies to everything from cleaning your oven to sacking your workforce.

CUT DOWN ON THE AGONY OF ANTICIPATION. GET ON WITH IT

Nothing succeeds like success. When you have positive results to review, you feel hugely motivated to keep going. When an individual or a team gets into the 'winning habit', it often seems that everything they do seems destined to go their way. We see it when tennis players are 'in the zone' and every serve is an ace. It was evident in the Manchester United Treble winning team of 1998–99, where the group as a whole was so galvanized that it became greater than the sum of its component parts. We witness it in the smile on Delia Smith's face as she draws yet another perfect soufflé out of the oven. The positive, success-oriented mindset conferred by success helps generate further success.

Planning is crucial, but let's not forget the role that luck sometimes plays in success. Indeed, many game of life winners refer to the part that luck has played in their good fortune by placing them in the right place at the right time. Luck, however, is rarely mere accident.

> Luck is what happens when preparedness meets opportunity.

In outlining what he calls his Circle Theory, Sir Martin Sorrell, Chief Executive Officer of WPP, suggests that the harder you work, the more you see, the more people you meet, the more situations you encounter. In other words, the more circles you move in, the more likely you are to collide with different opportunities and to be 'lucky'. But it's up to you, the individual, to make the most of those opportunities when they arise. Many people *have* opportunities, but how many *grasp* them? All the more reason to leave some room in your well-planned life to allow for the unexpected.

> Allow some space for spontaneity. Leave some leeway for Lady Luck.

Whatever your area of endeavour, you'll find it easier to make that decision and cut to the chase if you make sure you keep things simple.

'Long-windedness is often a smokescreen for woolly thinking,' observes Sir Martin Sorrell. 'If someone can't convince you that an idea is brilliant within five minutes, then, generally speaking, it's not that brilliant.'

The best game plan in the world counts for nothing if the ball doesn't end up in the back of the net. Keep your goal simple, and keep it clearly in mind. Then get on with the game and *shoot*!

CHAPTER SIX

sorry, offside!

Failure is a test of courage. There is always something to learn. One never stops learning, particularly when one is losing. When one loses, one knows what has to be done. When one wins, one is never sure.

Enzo Ferrari

However carefully you plan, and however hard you work, you'll still meet obstacles on the way to winning the game of your life. Dealing with setbacks may often seem difficult, but failure can often be turned into a positive experience. If you take the time to analyse, understand and assimilate what's happened, you can use the lessons you draw from failure to improve your self-knowledge. Everyone makes mistakes. Mistakes are part and parcel of human experience. Correctly interpreted, mistakes can help us towards gaining better judgement which, in turn, helps us to get things right next time. However hard it may seem at the time, try to treat every mistake or failure as an opportunity to learn and endeavour to keep things in perspective. When things go wrong, allow yourself free rein to feel down and depressed, but not for too long. Resolve to cut your losses, or try to put things right.

> Acknowledge the failure. Learn the lessons. Make the changes. Move on.

It's easy to feel disheartened when things don't appear to be going according to your game plan, but however bleak the situation, don't lost sight of your overall goal or vision. Remember that the wisdom you derive from overcoming your immediate obstacles may even help you reach your long-term goals more effectively. Remain constant to your vision, but flexible in your approach. Whatever happens, find some way of making apparent setbacks fit into your overall scheme. Take the example of Nelson Mandela. For most of us, the idea of spending years banged up in solitary confinement would not seem the ideal way for a political leader to run a national liberation campaign. For Nelson Mandela, however, that period of enforced contemplation was precisely what he needed to think through his plans for post-apartheid South Africa. Setbacks, when firmly linked to an overall plan, can often be turned to good effect.

> Whatever your immediate problems, continue to concentrate on the big picture.

Minor setbacks are the stuff of everyday existence (the missed train, the cancelled appointment, the overcooked roast), but how do you cope when things go seriously awry – when you've lost your job, your wife has left you, and now even the cat is packing. Whatever happens, don't start by asking yourself questions along the lines of 'Why am I such a complete and utter failure?' Rather, start by asking yourself *why* you lost your job. Which factors led up to it? Were these *external* factors, which were beyond your control (British manufacturing industry in generalized crisis due to overvalued sterling), or were they *internal* (your own chronic absenteeism)? Maybe you simply hated the job in the first place. It was never the job for you, and, sub-consciously, you always wanted to leave. Or perhaps, with hindsight, calling the boss a prat was not your brightest career move and, having recognized that, you resolve to watch your temper in the future. And as for the wife, maybe her family has a history of bolters and her disappearance is no reflection on you. Or perhaps your affair with her sister was not quite so clever after all and actually you had it coming.

However grim the situation, never fall into the trap of making sweeping generalizations. You may well have made a mistake – even a gross mistake – in one area of your life, but that doesn't mean that you're an out-and-out failure in every other area. True, as a lying, arrogant, self-obsessed, serial adulterer you may have to rethink your prospects as a country vicar. But, let's face it, there's always politics.

Whenever we're in the doldrums, it's easy to see everything in a negative light. The mere fact that someone fails to return a call, for example, begins to assume enormous significance in our minds. You begin to feel that you no longer count, that you're no longer a player, and that everyone thinks you're washed up. Obsessed with your own problem, you simply can't realize that the person who failed to return your call is probably up to his neck with problems of his own. His failure to call is no reflection on you, and yet you allow it to drag you down even further. Treat it as no more than it actually is: an unreturned call, nothing more!

> Keep negative emotions in hermetically
> sealed containers.

Never allow negative feelings in one area of your life spill over and poison every other area of your life. The fact that you flunked the exam, missed the turn-off on the motorway, burned the dinner or were rejected for the job, may well be a source of disappointment. But don't allow your disappointment to infiltrate every nook and cranny of your mind.

LEARN HOW TO COMPARTMENTALIZE

When confronted with failure, it's all too easy to give way to negative and destructive emotions which, if left unchecked, will undermine our fundamental wellbeing and inhibit our capacity to get on with life.

Anger

There was a time when anger, or 'letting off steam', was thought to be good for the system. Indeed, there was even some highly debatable research to suggest that people who failed to 'externalize' their negative emotions were more likely to suffer from cancer. Anger, however, is corrosive. Quite apart from the deleterious effects of angry outbursts on the poor people on the receiving end, uncontrolled outpourings of anger are a waste of time and energy for the individual involved. Within a group, such irascible behaviour may even destroy any semblance of team spirit.

Few of us are saints. We all feel angry from time to time, often with complete justification. The best reaction to anger, however, is not to 'take it out' on others – usually those who happen to be lower down the corporate or familial ladder. On the contrary, the healthiest response to anger is to acknowledge the feeling, admit that you're angry, accept that you have every right to be so, and then let it go. Don't allow the anger or the reasons for the anger to fester. Remember that nothing is more mentally and physically destructive than unresolved anger. The earlier you recognize and release your anger, the sooner you'll regain your enthusiasm for winning the game of your life.

Frustration

When confronted with failure or setbacks, we often fall prey to frustration. Frustration is the antithesis of enthusiasm. Nothing saps your energy more than the niggle of constant frustration – the feeling that you're not doing, or not able to do, what you really want to be doing in life. Once again, the solution to frustration lies in swift and honest acknowledgement of what is happening to you. If you feel frustrated in your job, for example, there's no point wasting the next twenty years of your life whingeing about it. Take control. Recognize honestly and openly the need to make changes. Muster the guts to quit or start changing the job to suit yourself. Failing that, you could always start learning additional skills which might make the job more interesting. If none of these options is possible, then try to acquire coping skills such as tolerance and equanimity. Left unresolved, frustrations at home or in the workplace can swiftly lead to a breakdown in trust, communication, domestic harmony and team spirit. Whenever you're feeling frustrated, it's crucial to identify the causes and to hammer out a solution with colleagues or family members. The longer you allow the destructive weed of frustration to grow, the more embedded its roots become and the greater chance of its creating damage. Frustration, like all negative emotions, must be nipped in the bud.

Worry

In the face of adversity and even when your game plan appears to be working quite well, you may fall prone to worry. Everyone worries. Show me the person who doesn't worry and I'll show you the village idiot. Of course, a certain amount of worry is natural. It's only normal to be concerned about our health, our security, our children, our ageing parents, our environment and the parlous state of the England cricket team's lower order line-up. Worry, or at least a sensible and controlled amount of concern, is par for the course. Worry is what we experience when we consider the possible downside, when we look at the negatives of a given situation rather than the positives, when pessimism takes over from optimism and anxiety takes a grip. Like frustration and anger, worry must be dealt with as quickly as possible. The paralysis of acute anxiety is swift to set in and, with it, the whole raft of debilitating negative emotions. Deal with anxiety aggressively. Box it in. Ring-fence it. Refuse to allow it a parking permit in the recesses of your mind. Control it by granting it limited visiting rights for, say, one concentrated session each day. Then, during that session and *only* during that session, deal with it proactively. Don't just sit there fretting. Look at each problem objectively. Ask yourself whether the game is really worth the candle. If the answer is no, then axe that problem at once. Refuse to think about it any more. If, however, the problem is worth worrying about, then see what you can do to resolve it. Seek help from friends, colleagues or a professional. Do whatever you can to solve that particular issue and then move on. Whatever the result of your efforts, *keep on moving*. Worry thrives on stasis. Anxiety hates activity. Most worries simply cannot cling on once you have decided to shake them.

One friend of mine, a female consultant gynaecologist, has found an extremely effective method for dealing with worry. On her desk she keeps a box of matchstick-sized 'worry men'. Whenever she catches herself worrying, or she is confronted by a problem she can't resolve immediately, she shares the concern with a 'worry man' – effectively dumping the problem on him. She then disciplines herself to return to the 'worry men' at a specific, time-barred period of the day, and deals with the worries then. Thus instead of being controlled by her worries, she is in control of them. Rather than allowing her problems to infuse her thoughts, drain her energy and divert her attention from her highly demanding job, she literally and metaphorically 'boxes them in' until she elects to deal with them. By choosing a specific time to deal with worry, she not only controls her life but also maintains a positive mindset to deal with the critical decisions which confront her during the rest of her day.

Why not create your own personalized form of 'worry box'? Set aside a period each day to deal with your concerns and, during that period, consider each individual worry in turn. In fact, once you start doing this you'll probably find that a lot of your worries have managed to sort themselves out during the course of the day. For more serious concerns, seek the relevant help and support. Then let it go and leave it until your next appointed 'worry session'.

> Never allow the worm of worry to destroy the entire apple of your life.

Depression

Setbacks, especially serious setbacks, may often result in depression. The curse of depression is disturbingly prevalent nowadays, and most of us will have experienced the depression associated with the death of a loved one, the loss of a job, or the failure of a marriage or a relationship. This reactive form of depression is perfectly natural and, painful though the condition is, will usually improve our time. (Endogenous depression, the form of depression for which causes are not immediately apparent, is far more difficult to deal with and professional medical help is advised.)

The feeling of utter dejection associated with depression – 'the wind of the wings of madness' – is never to be underestimated. Loss of interest, appetite, energy, enthusiasm and, in extreme cases, even the will to live are all symptoms of the condition. In many cases, however, it doesn't matter how low you're feeling, you can do something to alleviate the symptoms of depression.

Apart from medical treatment and psychological counselling, the first absolute 'must' is exercise. (Regular exercise is of course crucial for everyone's physical and mental wellbeing, whether or not they're feeling depressed.) Exercise, even in the form of a brisk walk, helps to maintain or gain fitness. In turn, this feeling of physical fitness reinforces a feeling of control, which helps to counteract the feelings of helplessness associated with depression. Many people find that the gesture of helping other people, often through volunteer work, or simply 'keeping busy' – even by doing something as trivial as tidying a cupboard – can also help overcome the feelings of lassitude and isolation often linked with depression. Whatever the failure, whatever the setback, you've got to grasp the nettle swiftly in order to allow enthusiasm back into your life. Only with enthusiasm can you return to your game plan and continue enjoying the game of your life.

In dealing with failure, you show your true mettle. Coping with success has its own problems, but in coping with failure you'll find yourself calling on some of the greatest human attributes – those of courage, patience, determination, adaptability and discipline. Whenever you're confronted with what seems like a problem, try and see it in a long-term context. In this respect, Michael Atherton, former England cricket captain and a man who's had his fair share of both bouquets and brickbats, emphasizes the importance of maintaining an even keel emotionally. 'When you're emotionally balanced,' he says, 'and that often involves blotting out a lot of what other people are saying, then it's much easier to cope in the ups and downs of life and to maintain that all-important perspective.'

> It doesn't matter if you lose the odd battle so long as you win the war.

The ultimate challenge in adversity is to keep on giving things your best shot and to maintain your faith with yourself. To paraphrase Kipling's celebrated poem, *If*, you must try and keep your head even when all about you are losing theirs. This may suggest, of course, that you haven't quite grasped the severity of the situation. But ideally, it will indicate that you have perspective and balance and, with that, the guts to persevere. Genius, intelligence, vision, energy – all these qualities are important in winning the game of your life. But can you summon the patience, determination and tenacity to continue when things are going wrong? Do you possess the requisite staying power?

> Whatever you're doing, and however bad it gets, you've got to have the crucial 'KBO' factor. The all-important 'Keep Buggering On' mentality.
>
> Sir Martin Sorrell, CEO, WPP

When you're playing to win the game of life and working with a game plan based on *your* desires and *your* aspirations, the greater will be the chances of your finding the discipline to remain committed to it. As a general rule of thumb, we always find the time and the energy to do what we *really* want to do, that's to say, what we consider *fun*. Most parents have experienced the 'too tired!' chorus when they ask their children to tidy up their bedrooms. But isn't it curious how the tiredness seems to evaporate instantly at the jingle of the ice cream van! In much the same way, if you find that you don't have the discipline to stick to your plan, it's probable that you didn't want the end result *badly enough*. You didn't want to lose weight *badly enough*. You didn't want to leave your job *badly enough*. You didn't want to quit those ghastly cigarettes *badly enough*.

One highly effective way of reinforcing discipline is by harnessing the powerful amalgam of pressure, compassion and understanding exercised by support groups such as Weight Watchers and Alcoholics Anonymous. The fear of failure in the eyes of a sympathetic peer group is usually a strong motivating factor in maintaining discipline, and there's no doubt that these organizations work admirably for certain types of game plan.

Not all plans, however, have such focussed and relevant support groups. If your plan is tailored specifically for *you* and *your* needs, you may find yourself on your own when it comes to maintaining both discipline and momentum. The key to discipline is to convince yourself that you want something *desperately*. If you visualize the end result in forceful, positive and attractive terms, it becomes irresistible which, in turn, encourages discipline. Remember that positive images are always more powerful than negative ones. As a simple example, stop saying 'I don't want to be unfit and constantly weary.' Instead, paint a mental picture of yourself springing out of bed in the morning, smiling as you pull on your tracksuit and trainers, and breathing in the fresh morning air as you hail fellow joggers in the park. Since it posits a clearly defined goal, 'I want' will always be an infinitely more powerful message than the far more nebulous 'I don't want'.

Patience, of course, is an essentially personal reaction to any given situation. Patience is your capacity to demonstrate tolerance and perseverance in the face of stress, difficulty or adversity. In your efforts to 'Keep Buggering On', however, you'll often find that you and your reactions are not the only factors in the equation. In managing any new situation, you must also exhibit some understanding of how your growth, change and behaviour is going to impact on those around you. How are *they* going to cope with the new, or the projected new, situation? Others may be feeling nervous, uneasy or even threatened by any shift in the status quo and, if you are going to enlist their support, you can't simply ignore these fears. Your sensitivity to other people's issues is often vital to your overcoming setbacks and continuing on the road to success.

CHAPTER SEVEN

you'll never walk alone

Walk on, walk on with hope in your heart
And you'll never walk alone

Traditional and Liverpool FC anthem

Whatever situation you're dealing with, be it triumph or disaster, it's crucial to involve all the key people in your life. OK, so you've been kicked out of your job as a VAT inspector, you've overcome the initial depression associated with this rejection and now you've decided to use the opportunity to fulfil your long-term dream of scaling Mount Everest. All very well. But have you stopped to discuss the details of your new game plan with your wife or husband? Have you considered your children's fears about the imminent prospect of penury and homelessness?

Whether personal or professional, the success of any new game plan is dependent on the involvement, the input and, ideally, the support of all the individuals who have a stake in the game of your life. These key stakeholders may be your family, friends, employer, business partner, team-mates, bank manager – whoever. The more fully key stakeholders feel they've been consulted in the formulation of your plan, and the more they feel they've been allowed to make some positive contribution, the more likely they are to accept the plan and help you bring it to fruition.

> Don't court failure upfront by going it alone.
> Whatever you do, get the whole team on your side
> before you do it.

No man is an island. Unless you're a self-employed, genius-hermit living in a cave, you're going to need family, friends, partners, employers or neighbours to help you cope with setbacks and move forward with your game plan. Your requirements may be simple: 'I'm slipping up on my diet, so please hide the biscuits' or 'It's really no use: I can't stop boozing. Please throw away the corkscrew!', or more complicated: 'I just can't reach this target all on my own. Please support me in raising the funds for the new school hall.' We often forget that most people are so involved in running their own lives that, unless we actually ask for their help, they rarely guess our need for it. So go ahead and ask! At worst, your request will fall on deaf ears and at best, you'll be given all the help you need.

In dealing with setbacks, we're often tempted to withdraw into our metaphorical shell to consider our next move. There's nothing wrong with this, provided it doesn't continue for too long. You're not going to move forward by cutting yourself off from the very people who're going to help and support you through this difficult patch. When we ourselves are feeling down, it's all too easy to ignore the needs of those close to us. And yet now is the very time that they need consideration.

Efforts to move forward after adversity often come as a shock and, therefore, a threat to the people around. Take the example of one woman I spoke to recently: faced with her husband's redundancy, she took it upon herself to sign up for a secretarial course before finding herself a job. Far from being pleased and relieved at this development, the husband went into decline. Having been used to being the major breadwinner with a wife at home, permanently available and catering to his every need, he suddenly found himself left to deal with the dreary domestic demands of the family. The poor man felt decidedly threatened by the prospect of his wife going out to work. Perhaps her new-found financial independence would change her attitude to him? Perhaps she'd fall for a more attractive man in the office? Quite apart from this, he didn't feel that it was a man's job to do the shopping, cook the evening meal, and organize the children's homework.

In navigating treacherous waters, you must communicate your strategy to the rest of the crew well in advance of the rapids. Discuss the problems and the setbacks openly. Encourage others to discuss the ramifications of the tack you intend to take. Listen to people's concerns and objections. The changes you want to make will, by definition, demand reorganization, maybe even upheaval, so try to explain why you've decided to do what it is you're going to do.

Take the example of another friend of mine, a mother of three, who decided that she wanted to return to work. Just like the lady in the previous example, she met with quite some resistance from her husband. My friend, however, handled things better. She explained that, with the children growing up, she felt that the household budget needed the injection of the additional cash her new job would create. This argument he rejected. After all, he argued, they were doing all right on his salary. The family wanted for nothing. It was then that she mustered the courage to express the growing unhappiness and frustration she felt, sitting at home watching her many skills and talents as a television producer atrophying. At last, he began to understand, and then support her in her plan.

Dealing with adversity often involves subtle, occasionally even radical, changes in direction and any change in direction is bound to create problems. In order to alleviate these tensions, you must agree on a coping strategy, and put it into place. Take the example of my friend, the television producer: once the decision to return to work had been reached, she invited all members of the family to help her draw up a household schedule. Each individual was allotted specific tasks. Her teenage children who, up until that point, had assumed that dirty clothes left strewn across the floor simply reappeared washed, ironed and nicely hung, were swiftly disabused of their apparent belief in fairies. They learned how to use the washing machine, and now they understand the bore of ironing, and are rather more careful about hanging up their clothes. Even her husband (not exactly the New Man prototype) is playing ball. Relieved that the financial burden of the family no longer lies entirely on his shoulders, he's begun to understand the logic of sharing some of the domestic chores. He's also thrilled to have a wife who is now happy, energetic and looking ten years younger.

Disappointments are sent to try us and, with luck and good management, we emerge from the experience stronger and wiser. When your entire game plan seems to be collapsing around your ears, however, you're bound to find the experience unnerving, and the odd disagreement or even crisis is inevitable. With communication, cooperation and good will, however, most problems can be dealt with effectively. However large or small the change necessitated, whether it's a proposed return to work or the reorganization of a major multinational company, it's important to recognize that this change can't occur in a vacuum. Try and enlist the support of allies and, where people are affected by your change, help them to understand the issues involved, help them accept the inevitability of this change and encourage them to adjust.

> If failure is a test of courage, then principle is the weapon which will help us withstand that test.

There was once a woman who passionately believed that the policy of animal testing, then prevalent in the multibillion-dollar cosmetics industry, was immoral and unacceptable. She resolved to offer the public an alternative: beauty products which did not involve animal testing and which were both environmentally and ecologically friendly. With a minuscule bank loan, she set up a small shop in Brighton and, having survived the initial adversity of cash flow problems, went on to become one of the major success stories of the 1980s. That woman was Anita Roddick, and the fundamental tenets of her Body Shop philosophy became so widespread that they're now considered mainstream. It was because her marketing policy was not simply a gimmick, but a deeply rooted belief based on firmly held principles, that she found the determination to overcome the initial, financial obstacles and achieve her resounding business success. At the same time, her perseverance made her a protagonist in the campaign to raise public awareness of the environmental and animal right issues which were of such concern to her. Roddick and her principles succeeded in changing the way most women think about cosmetics.

> Do you have the courage to be guided by your own
> principles even in adversity?

Unlike suffragettes, martyrs and a few extraordinary individuals such as Martin Luther King, Nelson Mandela and Mahatma Gandhi, few people espouse their principles so fervently that they are prepared to die for them. But do you at least have the courage to be *guided* by your principles? Are you prepared to work for a boss whose remarks are overtly racist? Do you have the guts to leave a dead-end relationship which you know is dragging you down? Are you prepared constantly to put your work before your relationships? Decide which of your own principles are non-negotiable. Refuse to compromise on these, but realize that although the 'end' you have in sight is non-negotiable, you're allowed all the freedom you need to make alterations to the 'means' to that end. In the game of life, elements of even the best-laid plans may go astray and you may find that some fine tuning is in order. Without losing sight of your ultimate objective, always feel free to be flexible in your approach.

It's important to recognize the point at which adversity demands a change in direction. Take the example of a neighbour of mine who resolved to get to grips with Information Technology and, with the full support of her family, signed up for a six-month intensive course at night school. The course involved three nights per week and a substantial amount of homework. The course was going swimmingly and her grasp of IT was improving by the day. However, the downside was that things at home were suffering. Her husband was under enormous pressure at work and was returning home later than usual. In addition, without her mentoring presence, her children's homework was falling by the wayside.

Imagine this woman's dilemma. Should she rigidly stick to her objective and refuse to be deflected from her ambition of learning something new and useful? Should she give up completely? Or should she opt for a less intensive course, involving one evening a week, which would allow her to reach the same objective, albeit within the context of a longer time-frame? After careful consideration, she decided to make a few modifications to her original plan and continued with the less intensive course. By demonstrating fairness and flexibility, she managed to accommodate the needs of every family member concerned.

There will always be a crunch-point, however: an issue on which you absolutely refuse to compromise. In the example of this woman, she was prepared to be flexible on the timetabling of her plan, but she was not prepared to compromise on her goal of learning about IT. The modalities may have been altered, but the ultimate objective had not.

What if your goal is to lose fourteen pounds in weight? You've set yourself a reasonable weekly target of losing two pounds per week for seven weeks. However, you're finding it hard to concentrate at work because of constant hunger pangs. In fact, your goal is so ambitious that you're beginning to lapse and your occasional binges are making you feel disheartened. Now's the time to reappraise the situation. After a more realistic assessment of your target, your lifestyle and your own personality, you may decide that a weight loss of one pound per week over fourteen weeks is a more reasonable plan for you. Again, although the terms of the plan have been altered to accommodate a few minor glitches, your focus on the ultimate goal continues to be maintained.

Whatever you're doing, remember to keep on communicating! Communicate with those people whose help you'll need in implementing your game plan, or who'll find themselves affected by it, and *continue* to keep them informed when you have to make adaptations. If people don't know what's happening, how can they help you? Once again, depending on the objective you're trying to achieve, you may have to involve your family, colleagues, team-mates or even bank manager. Perhaps your business plan and your profit forecasts were a trifle over-optimistic. Now you're experiencing cash flow problems and are concerned about making pay-roll. Don't hide your head in the sand. Far better to take the bull by the horns, explain the situation to your bank manager and tell him how you intend to improve it. If you fail to keep him patched in, things will only deteriorate further. Involve him. Seek his help. Ask for his support. Invite his suggestions. And one more thing – ensure that you owe him a veritable packet. Then your inability to repay the fortune becomes *his* problem, not yours.

Of course, flexibility does not mean changing everything at the first sign of difficulty. The need for a bit of fine tuning is not an excuse for throwing in the towel at the slightest mishap. Learn how to monitor and adjust your game plan. Remain adaptable, but at the same time strive to retain focus.

Most worthwhile objectives in life involve sacrifice. In order to focus on winning the game of your life, you may find you have to make certain changes in your current lifestyle. Let's say you want to be fit and healthy in order to enjoy your life more. You know you've been eating, drinking and smoking too much and now you're getting pains in your chest. Without the doctor having to tell you, you realize you've got to quit. Unfortunately, your entire social scene revolves around meeting your mates in the pub where several rounds, a packet of fags and a takeaway is par for the course. Now you're wondering how you're going to stick to your new regime of salad and mineral water and still go out in the evening. You're worried that your friends will laugh and call you a killjoy. So, what are you going to do?

It all depends on you. If you have a will of steel, you'll still be able to meet up with your old friends in the pub while sticking to your new-found straight and narrow. More likely, you'll have to set about constructing a different lifestyle which is not based entirely on booze and baltis. To fill in the social void and, at the same time, move towards your given objective, you might even decide to join a health club and start exercising every evening.

Without constant monitoring, however, it's easy to lose focus. Little by little, you find your resolve to achieve a certain goal begins to fade. You become easily distracted. Instead of sticking to your own agenda, you find yourself being sidetracked. Just the odd biscuit, just the odd pint, just the odd missed deadline or the odd lesson unattended. When you notice this happening, don't be too hard on yourself. The odd slip-up is not the end of the world. Provided that it's swiftly acknowledged, it doesn't mean that your game plan has come apart at the seams. Don't allow one false move, one mistake or one bad day to put you off course completely. Recognize, reappraise and refocus.

No scuba-diver would ever dive without a 'buddy'. Whenever there's a problem, your buddy is always there for you and you're always there for your buddy. In the game of life, we all need a buddy. Whatever you're trying to accomplish, it's easier to achieve it with a buddy. Whenever there are storm clouds on the horizon, it's easier to confront them with a buddy. Try and find someone who, in moments of crisis, will encourage or embarrass you into picking yourself up, dusting yourself down and starting all over again.

Be sure to choose buddies who will facilitate your ability to focus on your overall goals. Conventional support networks (Weight Watchers, Alcoholics Anonymous etc.) suggest regular attendance at meetings in order to applaud progress and monitor recidivism. Other networks are not so effective in supporting their members. As a working mother, I've often found that the effort involved in creating a support network is so exhausting that I've barely got the energy to complete the task for which I needed a support network in the first place. Make sure that the game is worth the candle. If your support network is deflecting you away from your objectives rather than helping you focus on them, reassess the situation. I know one working mum who spent two months trying to humour a homesick au pair. In the end, the girl returned home having done nothing whatsoever except run up a three-hundred-pound phone bill!

The concentrated push you often need in order to succeed in one area of your life may well disturb the balance you need in other areas. One man I interviewed for this book decided to leave his well-paid City job to set up a business on his own. He soon found himself working far longer hours, devoting his weekends to the new business and having less time available for himself, family, friends and leisure pursuits. He recognized the problems but decided that, in the short term at least, the sacrifice was worth it. Gradually, however, the short term became a little longer. The business took off and began to take over his life completely. The business and his desire to develop it further became an all-consuming obsession. Always a hard-working man, he fell prey to absolute workaholism which, while the most acceptable of all the 'isms' in a capitalist society, was nonetheless an unhealthy obsession.

Three years down the road, he found that the reasons why he wanted to start his own business in the first place (more autonomy, more leisure, more time with the family) had become completely obscured. Only when his wife (a woman of limited imagination) waltzed off with her tennis coach did he start to question his own behaviour.

Whatever your goal, ask yourself 'Is it worth it?' Think of all the sacrifices you'll have to make in order to achieve it. Is the effort involved worth the degree, the gong, the medal or the feel of that small child's arms around your neck? If your answer isn't a resounding 'Yes', then it's time to think again.

Working through adversity and making changes to your game plan are difficult and challenging exercises, but you'll be rewarded for the effort.

Although establishing your own personalized plan requires time and thought, the discipline will give your life purpose and meaning. A game plan enables you to organize and implement the changes that either adversity or new developments oblige you to make in your life. In addition, clearly understood goals provide you with a very powerful guiding force. It doesn't matter whether your objective is passing your driving test or acquiring your PhD. Even when you find yourself confronted by setbacks, a plan will continue to give you impetus. It will propel you towards success. Remember, your game plan and its goals are the only yardstick you have to determine whether or not you're winning the game of life. Without a plan, you're potentially missing many opportunities, both personally and professionally. Can you really afford not to take the time to create your own plan?

> Life consists not so much in holding good cards, but in playing those you hold well. Good cards or bad cards, you owe it to yourself to make the most of your hand.

CHAPTER EIGHT

your best shot

We are what we do repeatedly. Excellence, then, is not an art,
but a habit.

Aristotle

The story goes that Larry Bird, the great Boston Celtics basketball star, was once employed in a soft drinks commercial. For the purposes of the advertisement, Bird was called upon to miss a shot. Simple enough in concept, but the execution of his 'miss' proved far more difficult to deliver. The problem was that the player himself was *wired to win* and, as an increasingly impatient film crew hung around watching, he continued to score basket after basket. Despite the requirements of the script, he just could not bring himself to miss. Bird was, quite simply, conditioned to excellence. For him, as for any true champion, excellence had become a habit. Endless hours of practice and repetition had left him no alternative. Bird just had to give it, quite literally, 'his best shot'. His only option was to try his hardest; excellence was his only alternative.

Most of us can sparkle sporadically, but the secret of true excellence lies in consistency, in habitually doing well. In any sphere of endeavour, the pursuit of excellence is a *systematic and relentless process.*

> You get what you rehearse.

Winning teams such as Manchester United FC, FC Bayern Munich, the Chicago Bulls and the Atlanta Braves continually rehearse success. In the world of elite sport, natural talent is clearly essential, but talent alone will never be sufficient. It is the potent combination of talent and determination which marks out teams and individuals as winners. Champion golfer Nick Faldo famously went back to 'school' to deconstruct his swing in the endless pursuit of perfection. Excellence is never satisfied. It demands extraordinary and consistent levels of commitment. It demands that we constantly give life our best shot.

The great Formula One racing champion, Juan Mañuel Fangio, once said that 'You must always believe you will become the best, but you must never believe you have done so.' An outstanding competitor, Fangio recognized that complacency is the greatest threat to excellence and that *maintaining* high standards of performance is the most difficult challenge of all. Game of life winners also recognize that without new, exciting and ever more demanding goals, boredom and an acute sense of anticlimax may swiftly follow any success. Screeds have been penned on 'Astronaut Syndrome' – the phenomenon observed in certain individuals who, having achieved a lifelong ambition, fall prey to a 'What Now?' depression. Sir Edmund Hillary, the first man to scale Everest and a man who knows a thing or two about peak performance, also identified this phenomenon. The remedy lies, he believes, in constantly setting new targets for himself and dreaming up new challenges. Standing on the top of Mount Everest and having reached the top of the world in every sense, he might justifiably have wallowed in his moment of triumph. Instead, he found himself looking east to the unclimbed summit of Makalu and started instinctively picking out a route by which that mountain could be climbed. Hillary knew that the key to maintaining his own high standards lay in the constant search for new and exciting challenges.

In the world of sport, excellence is easy to recognize and measure. A glimpse at the league tables or the medal charts is all that's required. In everyday life, excellence is far more difficult to quantify and yet we all know it when we see it. Excellence need not be earth-shattering. Excellence may reside in a telephonist's helpful manner, a shop assistant's caring attitude, a builder's punctilious snagging, or a hotel maid's impeccably made bed. Everyone has the opportunity to excel. Anyone who resolves to go that proverbial extra mile in doing whatever it is they do is already on the road to excellence.

Many of us have self-imposed standards, our own individual 'personal best' against which we judge our own behaviour or performance. If we exceed those standards, we feel happy. If we fail to live up to them, we experience the discomfort of 'letting ourselves down'. These standards may appear banal (a cake that rises, a garden neatly trimmed), but that's of no consequence. Whatever they may be, standards are important because they provide an essential yardstick for measuring our behaviour and personal development. Without standards, you can't really decide if you're winning the game of life.

> Without standards, the value of 'Me PLC' stock is impossible to track.

SELF-IMPOSED STANDARDS

In order to identify your own self-imposed standards, you must first identify what's truly important to you. You may think, for example, that it's important to respond to deadlines, to set a good example to others and to be punctual. You may believe that only the best will do and that there's always room to achieve more. Determination and perseverance may be your guiding lights, or a belief in the need to show compassion and decency to other people. You may identify with the old adage that if a job's worth doing, it's worth doing well. Or you may even decide that all-round excellence is an impossible ideal and that, in reality, not everything you do can merit the 'Five Star' treatment.

Given the multiplicity of roles most of us are required to play, you may elect to set high but reasonable standards, to concentrate on the important things being done well and recognize that to excel in the 'Art of the Possible' is also a form of excellence. You may even share in my general philosophy:

- To be there for my *family and friends*.
- To do as well as I can in my area of *work*.
- To do as much good as I can for the *wider community*.

Take time to consider your own self-imposed standards. Then ask yourself the question: 'Am I living up to them?' If so, fine. If not, are you capable of doing more? Or are you happily stagnating in your comfort zone, doing just enough to get by? In other words, are you giving the game of life your very best shot? Can you find the energy to excel?

FIND THE ENERGY TO EXCEL

Know and Develop Your Own Special Ability, and Deploy it with Firm Commitment

Self-knowledge is all-important. Once you've hit upon your own very special vein of gold, concentrate on mining that seam! Focus on what you do best. What you do best tends to be the things you enjoy doing most and for which you'll always find energy! You may not believe that your talents are particularly mind-blowing, but who knows! Witness how far Bernard Matthews has gone on the back of a turkey! Identify what you can do, determine to do it to the best of your ability, and you're bound to be a winner.

Why is it, though, that some people *have* determination and others *don't*? Is it simply that the people who show little determination are not doing what they like doing (and therefore ought to be doing), whereas those who are determined are correctly focussed? Is determination inherent? Or can it be learned? Dr Liz Nelson believes that there is a 95 per cent correlation between determination and success. Determination, however, is heavily dependent on energy levels, which tend to be inherited, but they can also be influenced by lifestyle. It's important to understand this link because, in trying to achieve anything, determination is far more important than pure ability. Lifestyle choices are therefore crucial. The way we choose to function physically and mentally can dramatically influence our energy levels.

Create a Positive Mindset

We don't see things as *they* are, we see them as *we* are.

Anaïs Nin

It's hard to see hope with a hangover.

P. J. O'Rourke

Few of us will be called upon to run a four-minute mile, bat all day in the searing heat against the Australians, or turn around the fortunes of an ailing multibillion-pound corporation. We are more likely to understand the challenges of everyday life: the worries involved in looking after chronically ill parents and demanding children; the insecurity of short-term contracts; self-employment or continuous, often radical, change in working patterns; the daily, weekly and monthly hassle of balancing the family budget; and the fears associated with growing old, being alone and falling sick. Our worries are often more nebulous. Family doctors, overwhelmed with middle-aged men and women laid low with 'TATT' (Tired All The Time) syndrome, recognize the symptoms of stress and burn-out classically associated with the much laughed-at, but totally unfunny, phenomenon of midlife crisis. Once we stop seeing life in optimistic terms, we start to feel physically drained. Fatigue, stress, worry and burn-out are all debilitating conditions due to *energy deficiency*. When we're short on energy, everything is impossible. The simple act of getting out of bed in the morning is transformed into a herculean task. The prospect of the weekly shopping trip to the supermarket fills us with dread. The once enjoyable and productive commute to work degenerates into an unbearable daily grind.

A healthy lifestyle including a balanced diet, plenty of exercise, reasonable amounts of sleep and a fair split between work and leisure may alleviate the worst of these symptoms. More important than any physical change, however, is a change in mental attitude. In many cases, energy and vitality have very little to do with age and situation. Often, they are inextricably linked to an individual's view of life and his determination to see things in a positive light. The combination of energy and determination which flow from a positive mental attitude singles out the winners from the losers in the game of life.

When your mind is bored, you have no energy. You tire easily and everything is an uphill struggle. When your mind is alert and interested, your energy levels rise and even the most difficult of challenges is accepted with vigour. Find something you absolutely *love* doing. Throw yourself into it. Have faith in yourself and your own ability to master it. The more you love it, the more you lose yourself in it, the more energy you'll have for other areas of your life, too.

Refuse to Accept Defeat

You get what you anticipate, so *never* expect defeat. Sir Martin Sorrell often refers to the 'Dr Deaths' of an organization, i.e. the professionals who are paid to look at the potential downside of any action or decision. The Dr Deaths search for obstacles and problems. Their presence is unquestionably useful for stimulating debate and generating analysis, but their negativity must never be allowed to paralyse a company and arrest its growth. In our own make-up, we all have our Dr Death who lives in close proximity to our personal Pollyanna. While they are often at variance, Dr Death must never be allowed to win. Faith in your own ability, courage to carry things through, and a liberal measure of hard work all combine to form a potent mixture which will normally shift the most stubborn of problems. Once you determine to face up to your problems or even better, think about them logically and attack them aggressively, you'll find many of them disappear. Once you focus on your ability, rather than your inability, to cope with an obstacle, you'll start to convince yourself that this problem is not as intractable as you first imagined. Problems are only problems because you empower them with the title of 'problems'. Call them challenges. Call them opportunities. Call them the stuff of life, if you wish but, whatever you do, do not confer on them the status of problems. Every day we witness countless examples of people who refuse to allow their physical handicaps ruin their lives: the blind man successfully negotiating the busy road with his stick; the woman with MS bringing up happy, healthy, well-cared-for children; the jockey with cancer who fights his way back to health – the world is full of inspirational individuals who demonstrate that problems exist, first and foremost, in the mind. Believe that you *can* cope and you *will* cope. Believe you *can* win and you *will* win. Believe you *can* succeed and you *will* succeed. Always keep a clear picture of success firmly etched in your mind. There's no greater guarantee of achievement.

It May Seem Impossible But It Needn't Be Hard

Life is complicated enough without going out of our way to create extra difficulties. And yet when we're confronted with a problem, how often do we allow it to grow in our minds by chewing over every conceivable angle rather than cutting straight to the solution! Just as unsubstantiated rumours in the media are given 'legs' by Draconian gagging measures, so issues which could be dealt with directly, swiftly and painlessly are often puffed up out of all proportion by pointless over-reaction. Nothing is more energy-sapping and yet how often is it allowed to happen? We've all watched those deeply depressing television documentaries on 'neighbours at war' where a minor niggle is allowed to escalate into full-scale pitched battle. Fortunes are lost in increasingly bitter legal wrangles when a civilized conversation over a cup of tea might easily have settled the matter. How often are we incensed by a workman who promise faithfully to come at a certain time and then fails to show up? How often have we been exasperated by the classic 'the cheque's in the post' routine? And how much easier it would be for all concerned if people adopted the simplest route of all, that of honest communication. If only the overloaded workman would ring and explain his predicament. If only the hassled businessman would call to explain his temporary cash flow problem. Most people prefer the courtesy of the truth, however unpalatable, to the frustration of being either led up the garden path or left in the dark. The best way out of any problem is generally the simplest: Admit it, sort it, leave it. Have the courage to deal with problems swiftly and then move on. Conserve your energy. Use it wisely. It's far too precious to be wasted worrying.

CHAPTER NINE

keep working at it

Genius is one per cent inspiration and ninety-nine per cent perspiration.

Thomas Alva Edison

No one achieves success, either personal, professional, spiritual or emotional, without working at it. You may work hard, or *think* you work hard, but are you working *effectively*? You may put in all the hours God sends, insist on ploughing on through lunchtime, arrive in the office early and go home late and still be inefficient. You may refuse to accept your full quota of annual leave, consistently take work home in the evenings and note, with increasing despair, the diminishing returns on your efforts. The nation's cemeteries and coronary care units are tragically full of 'hard-working' people. So how can you turn your hard work into more effective work?

> Effective work may still be hard work; the beauty is
> that there's less of it.

TACTICS FOR GETTING THINGS DONE

Time Management

Do you ever feel pushed or stretched? Do you ever wake up, consider all the things to be done in the day and groan before diving back under the duvet? Are you suffering from compassion fatigue? When you watch the news on television, do you feel overwhelmed by the images of cruelty, suffering and famine and do you start to agonize over which, of the thousand heart-renderingly worthy causes making calls on your purse-strings, you ought to support? Do you ever feel that the whole world – family, friends, colleagues, even people with no legitimate claim on you – are constantly making demands, eating into your day and deflecting you from your purpose?

If you're feeling frustrated, stressed or depressed, the chances are that you're no longer simply stretched, but positively overloaded. You're not managing your time. And if you're not proactively managing your time, you're either doing nothing or, more probably, you're being *dumped* on.

'Dumpers' and 'Dumpees'

All the world's a stage, but you'll end up with a bit part in someone else's play if you don't put some thought into your own casting. Fail to organize your own agenda, fail to decide what you want to do, and you'll soon find yourself caught up in the drift of any and everyone else's plans. Are you, for instance, the willing mum who's *always* ready to collect other people's kids from school and find that somehow, the one day you're in a fix, there's no one there to help *you*? Are you the bloke who *always* drives his mates home from the pub and yet, the evening *you* want to celebrate with a few drinks, you discover that no one else is prepared to run the risk of staying sober? Or maybe you're the only secretary in the pool who's forever working late because the boss can trust *you* and *only you* with all the important stuff. Or are you the stressed-out salesman obliged to work twice as hard as his colleagues to make targets because only *you* have the charm to deal with the awkward customers? Does this sort of story sound familiar? If so, then you're a classic 'dumpee'.

The world is divided into three distinct categories. The first category comprises a relatively small group of 'self-reliers' – people who ask no one for anything and manage to do everything for themselves. The vast majority of the population, however, falls into the second or third category: 'dumpers', those who dump on other people (the more conventional term is delegate, and 'dumpees', those unhappy souls dumped upon by more organized, more assertive, or just downright more exploitative dumpers.

Far be it from me to suggest that you turn selfish, self-centred and stroppy overnight. No one is advocating a mass walk-out of the nation's housewives, secretaries and home helps. There are crucial distinctions to be borne in mind within 'dumpeedom'. Whenever you allow other people, either through ties of affection, a contract of employment or your own personal commitment, to exercise legitimate or agreed claims on your time, then you are acting with freedom. Your own agenda involves *choosing* to help other people to implement their agenda and this is a noble calling. You are, in effect, a *happy* dumpee and therefore there is no reason for you to change your current behaviour. It's only when the element of free choice is removed that the trouble begins. It's then that you begin to feel frustrated or exploited and, quite possibly, experience the need for change. So how can you tell if you're an unhappy dumpee?

Exploitative Dumpitis

The symptoms of '*Exploitative Dumpitis*' (E.D.) are easily recognizable. If you're feeling tired, irritable, stressed or frustrated, the chances are that you are suffering from E.D. E.D. is the condition most commonly associated with not doing, or not being able to do, what *you* want to do. And historically (not surprisingly) it has been most prevalent in women. Nowadays, however, the disease is spread fairly evenly between the sexes. It is a serious complaint which can easily become a chronic disease as the self-preserving *No* muscles gradually atrophy completely. You know you're suffering from E.D. the minute you hear your intuition shouting *No* and your mouth simultaneously saying *Yes*.

How to combat E.D. and function more effectively

Make a list of things that frustrate you, hold you up, or cause you stress at work. Do you waste time in pointless meetings you feel obliged to attend and which are of no relevance to you? Do you spend too much energy 'covering your back', neurotically copying in everyone, even those who have no real interest in your project? Do you allow constant interruptions from the phone, fax or e-mail to deflect you from what you want to do? Do you allow colleagues excessive leeway to pester you with their concerns?

Next, make a list of things that hold you up, frustrate you or cause you stress at home. Do you feel that you are constantly tidying up after everybody else? Are you frustrated by a lack of structure in your children's homework, bedtime, meal times and television viewing habits? Are you too tired at weekends to organize some positive recreational activity for yourself? Are you annoyed by the endless stream of mates visiting your teenage son at all hours of the day and night? Are you beginning to feel that the pet rabbit's aspirations for self-fulfilment have become more pressing than your own? List everything that bugs you. Then determine to stop it happening.

> Be politely but persistently assertive. Learn to say 'No'. Remember, you're not obliged to make excuses. 'No' is a complete sentence.

Always Deal With The Worst Things First

In organizing your daily priorities, always bite the bullet and deal with the tricky issues first. If you don't, you'll feel them hanging over you, like the sword of Damocles, distracting your attention from other more important or more enjoyable pursuits. Just get them out of the way.

One chief executive I interviewed works for an organization which was involved in the successful takeover of another company. A few months after the takeover, he was given the unenviable task of informing a significant portion of the workforce that they were going to be made redundant. For days, the poor man agonized over how he was going to break the news. He flirted with endless combinations of management-speak euphemism (downsizing, re-engineering) with which he hoped to make the message more palatable. Try as he might, however, he just couldn't find a formula with which he was happy and, in the end, he gave up. Early one morning, he summed his courage, convened a meeting of the workforce and, in plain English, explained the company's detailed redundancy plans.

To his surprise, the entire workforce rose to their feet and cheered. Their spokesman explained that for months before the proposed takeover and for weeks after it, every single employee had been suffering stress due to the sheer uncertainty of the situation. Now that this chief executive had communicated the management's plans, everyone in the organization knew precisely where they stood. Even those who were about to be made redundant felt, while not pleased, relieved to know exactly what was happening.

> Free up your mind and enjoy your life. Deal with the worst things first.

Organize and Prioritize

Given the many conflicting and apparently urgent demands on your time, you may find it difficult to decide what your priorities are. If so, formulate a clear vision of what you want to accomplish, and organize your activity with this in mind. How you prioritize will depend on the end result you want to achieve. Create a clear vision of what you want to achieve. Commit to it. Work backwards to establish your daily priorities. Remain determined to achieve them by maintaining a clear vision.

Believe in the Value of What You're Doing

If you truly believe that what you're doing is important, you'll find the motivation to keep working at it. If it's valid, never underestimate the value of the task you're doing, even if it's something as banal as changing nappies or helping small children learn their tables. Often the less the recognition or remuneration, the greater the importance.

See Opportunities, Not Problems

Margaret Thatcher, so the story goes, consistently maintained that there were no such things as problems, only opportunities. One day, her favourite personal adviser arrived in her office: 'Prime Minister,' he said, 'I'm afraid we appear to have an insurmountable opportunity.' The story is doubtless apocryphal but it helps underline the truism that it's not what happens to you that counts, it's how you choose to react to it.

We all know examples of individuals who have managed to turn negatives into positives. Although tragically paralysed after a riding accident, *Superman* actor Christopher Reeve dismissed the understandable temptation to curse the fates and decided instead to use his high profile and charisma to focus world attention on the difficulties encountered, and discrimination suffered, by disabled people everywhere. His fierce determination not to 'give in' to his disability and not to allow it to deprive him of a life worth living has been an inspiration to countless others.

When you feel that you are grasping the opportunity to do something positive and not merely spending your time sorting out a problem, you feel energized. This feeling in turn reinforces the self-discipline necessary to bring those opportunities to a fruitful conclusion.

> Turn negatives into positives and feel the power of purpose.

Self-discipline

Working effectively means not only planning your time, but also maintaining the self-discipline to stick to that plan. Few of us demonstrate the absolute self-discipline, constant commitment and iron will to win demonstrated by top athletes. How many of us could even contemplate the rigorous regime: the punishing schedule of gruelling training whatever the weather; the deprivations of a 'healthy' diet; the relentless effort to improve strengths and eliminate weaknesses; the constant, critical self-analysis?

Obviously, very few of us aspire to such peaks of physical performance as a Daley Thompson or a Steve Redgrave. As individuals, however, we can all learn a lot from the holistic approach adopted by athletes who understand the need to work effectively on *every* area of self – physical, mental, emotional and spiritual – in order to perform at their best.

However gruelling, self-discipline comes more easily when you enjoy what you're doing. But what happens when you're confronted with doing something you don't want to do? Do you ignore it, hoping that it will just go away, or do you keep pushing it down to the bottom of the metaphorical pile? Perhaps you resort to the classic 'Didn't have time' excuse? Don't try kidding yourself. Not having time to do something simply means *not wanting to do it enough*. Can you find time to sample this rather fine bottle of Château Margaux? Can you find time to use these Cup Final tickets? Can you find time to go and choose yourself a new, top of the range BMW – courtesy of the company? Of course you can, because you *want* to. Can you find time to do those press-ups, floss those teeth, learn those irregular verbs, write that report, or muster the guts to get out of that dead-end job and find yourself another one? No? The reason is simply that you don't want to, or at least, that you don't want to *enough*.

We all have things we don't want to do. The difference between winners and losers in the game of life is that winners are prepared to do those things that losers refuse to do or drag their heels over doing. Winners don't particularly relish doing the unpleasant things either, but they're prepared to sublimate their dislike in an effort to reach their ultimate goal.

As children, we're soon introduced to the concept of deferred gratification. 'If you eat up all your greens, then you can have an ice cream.' In adolescence, the same concept is constantly reinforced. 'If you work hard at school and do well in your exams, then you'll end up with a good job.' And by adulthood, we are completely inured it. 'If you're prudent and save your money now, then you'll have a nice nest egg for your retirement.' In other words, if you do something rather unpleasant *now*, then as a guaranteed consequence you'll receive something much better *later*.

Human beings are amongst the few creatures in the animal kingdom able to grasp the concept of deferred gratification. *Let's face it, no one sells pensions to penguins.* A belief in 'jam tomorrow' is a powerful force for self-discipline. There are, however, far more proactive approaches to self-discipline than mere belief in a rosier future.

Motivate Yourself and Others

Motivation is closely allied to discipline. If motivation is the reason we do something combined with the impetus to do it, then discipline is the regime adopted to ensure that we continue doing it. Whereas discipline can always be learned, motivation seems to go far deeper. Why are certain people more motivated than others? Is it genetic? Is it cultural? Is it associated with stamina and energy levels? Or is it simply the way we're brought up?

Whatever the reasons, one fact remains. You can produce the most polished Power Point presentation on the planet, but you'll never succeed in motivating anyone else if you're not sincerely motivated yourself. By the same token, we usually need others in order to achieve our goals – whether it's organizing a successful children's picnic or the biggest takeover ever witnessed in the City of London.

How To Motivate Others

Paint passionate pictures

If you're not passionate about what you are doing, you'll never generate passion in anyone else. Politicians may try and fake it, but most of us can rumble their ersatz enthusiasm as swiftly as a spin doctor squashes sex scandals. Pseudo-enthusiasm leaves you cold. The real thing has you buzzing.

We can all remember those teachers whose enthusiasm held us in thrall and for whom we would happily try desperately hard. And we can all remember being bored witless by teachers who themselves seemed bored by the very subjects they were supposed to be teaching. To this day, my grasp of geography is decidedly dodgy – thanks to a teacher with a sharp line in sarcasm, an inability to recall our names, and a pronounced lack of interest in anything beyond sheep density in New South Wales.

Motivating people is not only crucial to the art of teaching but also to most other areas of our lives. Every time you want to encourage yourself or someone else to move towards a given objective, give your imagination free rein to create a vivid image of where you're heading.

> To motivate, use your imagination and your every sense to paint a truly passionate picture.

Make it match

In painting your passionate picture, make sure that the image depicted is relevant to you or to the individual you're trying to motivate. It's fatuous to conjure up compelling visions of walking to the North Pole when the person in need of encouragement is trying to increase sausage sales in Swindon. Ensure that your passionate picture strikes the right chord within the individual. Take the time and effort to make your picture person-specific.

> When the punter wants Picassos, don't give him Pollocks.

Rope in the rest

Everyone needs to feel needed and we all feel inclined to support projects in which we feel we have a stake. How many salesmen find their bright ideas consistently ignored? How many floor assistants know, better than any expensive squad of management consultants, why the line in luminous mango Lycra catsuits was a total and utter disaster? Game of life winners try hard to involve every individual in the team. They encourage everyone to add their contribution to the picture and, thus, to assume ownership of it.

> Turn the passionate picture into a collective collage.

Repeat, review and reinforce

It's important to keep the vision alive in your own and other people's minds. Continue to rekindle enthusiasm by constant reference to the overall picture. A one-off pep-talk is rarely enough to keep anyone going. We all need constant support and encouragement.

Locate the leverage

Different people respond to different stimuli. Many people seem motivated by money, although the truth is usually more complicated. Others by the desire for power or influence. Some may be moved by feelings of patriotism, guilt, pride, altruism, insecurity or duty. Others are spurred on by an interest in learning or personal growth; a commitment to the team or just blatant self-interest. Whatever it may be, everyone has some interest, belief or principle which informs their behaviour and decisions. The key to motivating people is to find what makes them tick. Inspire the soldier to fight for England, Harry and St George. Steer the footballer to success with visions of himself, his team-mates, his country and, if all else fails, lucrative sponsorship deals. Offer the salesman the trip of a lifetime to Rio. Bribe the children with Father Christmas. Promise yourself half an hour with your feet up watching *Countdown*.

The greatest leverage of all, however, is often a simple expression of trust. If you honestly say, 'I *trust* myself to accomplish this', you are demonstrating confidence in your own ability to do the job and creating an inner challenge to get it done. There are few more effective methods of self-motivation. Similarly, try telling other people that you trust them to do something. By assuming their competence, demonstrating your confidence and invoking their pride, you are creating massive leverage.

> Bait the hook to catch the fish.

Build belief

Have you ever watched a golfer who is suffering from the 'yips'? Or a footballer or cricketer who is 'out of form'? The golfer three-putts. The footballer misses open goals. And the cricketer is playing such horrible shots he's in danger of being selected for Middlesex. 'Form', and the loss of it, is intimately connected to confidence. 'In form' ice hockey players know not only where the puck is now, but where it is going to next. 'In form' batsmen see the ball ten times larger than it is. 'In form' tennis players know instinctively where that serve is going to land.

People on top form are brimming with confidence. Their confidence enhances performance which, in turn, generates success which, in turn, reinforces confidence which, in turn, generates even more success. As the old saying goes, nothing succeeds like success. And nothing builds self-belief more effectively than the constant rotation of a virtuous circle. But what happens when the opposite kicks in? An 'off' day produces a bad result, which leads to a loss in confidence, which leads to another bad day, which ends in further failure. Confidence plummets in a downward spiral as the vicious circle becomes entrenched.

When sportsmen and women are struggling, they often study videos of themselves in peak form. They recall memories of past victories, observe the things they once did right instinctively, and try to relive the feelings of euphoria associated with success. The power of these recollections can often help break the vicious circle. Once the first breakthrough has been made, confidence-building may resume.

Most of us don't have videos of ourselves performing in anything other than our brother's stag night or that office party we'd rather forget. Images of yourself gyrating to 'The Full Monty' or collapsed against the filing cabinet with Mr/Ms Marple of Marketing are probably not your best bet when suffering from a crisis of confidence. If this is the case, you'll have to work from memory alone. Try recalling every time you were successful at anything. If the crisis is chronic, or severe, you may be obliged to dig very deep: the toggle you were awarded for macramé at scouts, the goldfish with gout you won at the village fair. However trivial, give yourself a mental pat on the back for all your past successes. Soon, you'll discover that some of them weren't quite so trivial after all and that your list of successes is far more extensive than you'd imagined. A stockpile of positive, confidence-building memories is fundamental to our wellbeing. Be generous with yourself, then be generous to those around you! Add to other people's stockpiles by praising them honestly for their achievements. Seek out people who boost your self-esteem and try to steer clear of people who sap your energy by undermining your confidence.

> People can be divided into two categories: radiators and drains. Stick close to the radiators. Avoid the drains.

Factor in some fun

The important thing I have learned over the years is the difference between taking one's *work* seriously and taking one*self* seriously. The first is imperative, and the second is disastrous.

Dame Margot Fonteyn

The heavier the demands on your time, the more crucial it is to organize your time effectively and to cut out wasteful activity. It's important to remember that all work and no play makes Jack a dull boy. Factor some slack into your life. If there's no slack, how can you grasp those unexpected opportunities? If there's no slack, how can you ever relax, have fun, recharge your physical and mental barriers? Travelling by plane to New York, I once sat next to a man who turned out to be a major league tycoon. During the course of the flight, I couldn't help noticing the beautifully colour-coded time-management schedule to which he occasionally referred. I expressed my admiration and asked how he succeeded in organizing what was clearly a very busy life. He explained how he kept a daily and weekly schedule, then a rolling schedule which extended over the next three months, and yet another schedule which showed appointments booked over a year ahead. I noted that the most prevalent colour in the schedule happened to be blue and I asked him what that signified. The major league tycoon smiled a knowing, major league tycoon smile. 'The blue,' he replied, 'means holiday.'

Leisure time is important. More important still, however, is the ability to find fun in whatever it is we're obliged to do. Remember Mary Poppins, the mysterious nanny with magical powers who turned a dysfunctional group of individuals into a happy, cohesive, balanced family unit? The Poppins philosophy was simple: in every job that must be done, there is an element of fun. You find the fun and snap, the job's a game.

Most people with experience in dealing with small children are adept at transforming apparently irksome tasks into fun-filled activities. Thus learning how to count is transformed into a jewellery-making exercise involving brightly coloured beads. Learning how to measure becomes a joyous sand-slinging session and the children learn swiftly because they are having fun. Whatever you have to do, however irksome, try and find the upside.

> Find the fun in the job to be done.

Be wild and wacky when you want to be

> I love work. It fascinates me. I can sit and look at it for hours. I
> love to keep it by me: the idea of getting rid of it nearly breaks
> my heart.
>
> Jerome K. Jerome

Whatever happens, never shackle yourself so closely to any goal or plan that you miss the opportunity to meet new people, develop new relationships, or think creatively. Once you start feeling 'hemmed in' by over-scheduling, you run the risk of becoming stale and disaffected, and you'll find your self-discipline flagging. Remember, this is *your* game and these are *your* rules. Be wild and wacky when you want to be.

> Feel free to be flexible.

Pat yourself on the back

> I long to accomplish a great and noble task, but it is my chief
> duty to accomplish small tasks as if they were great and noble.
>
> Helen Keller

Always feel free to congratulate yourself on a job well done, whether it's finishing that daunting stack of ironing, or winning the Ladies Singles' title at Wimbledon. Find some small way of acknowledging your daily victories and of giving yourself a pat on the back.

> You're not a failure if you don't succeed, you're a success because you tried.

CHAPTER TEN

sick as a parrot, or over the moon?

People in the old times had *convictions*; we moderns only have *opinions*. And it needs more than a mere opinion to erect a Gothic cathedral.

Heinrich Heine (1797–1856)

Most people have beliefs. Unlike intelligence or ability, however, we can *choose* our beliefs. We can decide which positive, empowering beliefs we want to keep or acquire, and we can also decide which negative, restricting beliefs we want to ditch. Positive, empowering beliefs come in all shapes and sizes. You may choose to believe, like Sir Martin Sorrell, that 'Nothing is impossible once you elect to focus your time and energy and prioritize.'

Or you may draw strength, along with Sir Victor Blank, from your faith in the essential goodness of people. Or you may share the belief, espoused by both of these men, that the discipline of a set of religious ethics stands people in good stead both personally and professionally.

Whatever you choose to believe determines your behaviour. If you believe that you should do as you would be done by, you'll behave as a kind, concerned and socially responsible individual. If, on the other hand, you believe that life is simply a matter of dog eat dog, then kindness, concern and social responsibility won't feature too highly on your agenda.

Beliefs determine not only our behaviour but also how we feel about ourselves. The belief that we are worthwhile, valuable individuals will make us feel optimistic and 'Can do'. By the same token, the belief that we are worthless no-hopers will engender pessimistic 'Why bother?' feelings. We all, of course, have *opinions* (occasionally informed but often not) about the world around us. Opinions are fickle and may be changed at whim. Beliefs, however, have stronger roots and are far more deeply ingrained. Winners in the game of life find strength in a clearly defined set of beliefs.

Flirtatious and inconstant, Lady Opinion has her moments – but her influence is strictly limited. The annals of history are studded with examples of courageous people prepared to make the ultimate sacrifice, but never for anything as trivial as a mere point of view. Winners in the game of life are fuelled by something far more compelling than opinion. Winners, the sort of people whose actions and behaviour make a difference in life, demonstrate an inner strength which can only be conferred by belief. Nothing empowers us more than the force of true conviction. Nothing concentrates our minds and directs our behaviour more effectively than the guiding principles anchored in genuinely held beliefs. People without beliefs are like rudder-less vessels, without direction or compass, ready to be buffeted and blown wherever the prevailing wind will take them. Without a belief system, we are at the mercy of everything and everyone around us.

Winners in life succeed because they have the courage of their convictions. Think of Gandhi, a man who believed fervently in self-government for his native India, a man who believed that the racial injustices in his country should cease, but who also believed that any opposition to the imperial administration responsible for those injustices must be of a non-violent nature. Think of Mother Teresa, a woman who believed that even the poorest of the poor of Calcutta had the right to die with dignity. Think of inspirational leaders such as Nelson Mandela and Martin Luther King, men who were prepared to be imprisoned and die for their belief in the fundamental equality of all men and women. The radical changes they were instrumental in delivering were proportionate to the strength of their *convictions*.

Belief generates power. Self-belief promotes success. Think of heavyweight boxing legend, Mike Tyson, a man who doesn't know the meaning of the word defeat (granted, just one of the many words of which Mike Tyson doesn't know the meaning). Many would argue that such confidence stems from an uninhibited and unattractive killer instinct but, in the floor-or-be-floored environment of the boxing ring, that degree of self-belief is precisely what is required. The word 'self-doubt' can have no place in the lexicon of champions. In the game of life, winners recognize a negative thought as soon as it rears its ugly head and, like Tyson with a presumptuous opponent, will flatten it as soon as possible. Winners are not immune to occasional negative thoughts but, unlike their less successful colleagues, refuse to entertain them for long. Winners are adept at junking negative ideas as swiftly as possible and at replacing them with more positive and empowering thoughts.

Very few of us aspire to mix it with Mike Tyson. In our daily lives, however, we are constantly being called upon to give things our *best shot*. Life is often discussed in terms of a 'rat race'. Whether we like it or not, competition is all around us from the earliest age: competition to do well at school; competition to pass exams; competition to get a decent job, to earn a good living, to be promoted, to provide a happy home life. Sometimes the pressures and expectations seem overwhelming and, in such an eminently competitive world, nothing is more debilitating than the feeling that you are somehow not 'hacking it'.

Everyone has problems in life and an accumulation of difficulties can often be dispiriting. When this happens, it's all too easy to become caught in a downward spiral where nothing seems to go right. At work and at home, everything starts to look bleak – the chances are it will rain non-stop, your favourite football team will be relegated and, just when you think nothing else can go wrong, Liam Gallagher moves in next door.

It's precisely when things are looking at their worst that it's time to do some serious reappraisal. It's time (quite literally) to start counting your blessings. Nothing restores self-confidence and self-belief more effectively than a balance sheet of the pluses in your life. When the going gets really tough, don't make the mistake of writing lists of pluses *and* minuses in your life. The trouble with listing minuses is that, whenever you're feeling down, those same minuses stay etched in your mind. Somehow they seem to eat up your pluses, sap your energy and make you feel even worse. In critical fire-fighting situations, it's essential to ignore any negatives.

> Focus instead on all the positives in your life.

You may have a wonderful family who give you unconditional love and support. Or perhaps you have friends upon whom you can rely for help and advice. With luck, you've been blessed with good health. Whatever the positives, however small, write them down and focus on them.

The object of this exercise is to weigh all your assets in the balance. Take time out to understand just how important they are and how much good you really do have going for you. Seen against this backcloth of positive reinforcement, ask yourself whether it *really* mattered that you failed to get the job, the contract, or even the person you wanted to go out with. So what if you've been pipped at the proverbial post by someone better qualified, better prepared or even, heaven forbid, better looking than you! Once you've decided to change your 'I'm miserable' mind-set and once you've resolved to look at things with a positive mental attitude, you'll start to take all those apparent setbacks in your stride more easily. With a degree of healthy perspective, you'll understand and be able to reassess those apparently major problems for what they more realistically are: an inappropriate job, an impossible contract, and a ghastly man/woman you must have been bonkers to contemplate dating!

Winners in the game of life never allow individual setbacks to inform their entire outlook. The negative specific ('I've just lost my job') must never be allowed to become negative in general ('My life is a disaster'). A negative generalization is, without doubt, the best short cut to plummeting self-belief. No matter how serious the individual setback may be, it must be ring-fenced. The tumour of individual failure must be swiftly enucleated before it is allowed to spread. No one is pretending that this is always easy. In those dark moments which anyone of any insight or intelligence suffers, it may even seem impossible. If you're not careful, however, it's precisely at this point that the paralysis of depression may set in. If ever you feel this happening, remember that the imperative is to keep on trying.

Like a good relationship or a precious plant, self-confidence must be nurtured. It cannot be left alone in the pious hope that it will simply take care of itself. Belief in oneself, like physical fitness, needs constant practice. How often have we seen a top sportsman or sportswoman's self-confidence collapse after one bad game or match? In tennis, you can sometimes see it happening within the space of a point! Without a strong bedrock of self-belief, your confidence may easily be undermined. Winners in the game of life strive to ensure that self-belief is constantly reinforced and bolstered.

A few years ago, I worked with Daley Thompson, one of the world's greatest all-round athletes, and gold medal winning decathlete in both the 1980 and 1984 Olympic Games. Despite his success over the years, Daley's critics were never short on the ground. Many press commentators made constant play of the athlete's occasionally brash behaviour, and Daley's own insistence that any journalist wishing to interview him must first list (in correct order) the ten events of the decathlon did little to endear him to some. Outside the sporting arena, this same brash, arrogant and dismissive man was the epitome of fun, charm and good manners. Daley's apparent 'arrogance' was 'professional' not 'personal'. In the highly competitive world of international athletics it was, for him, a necessary externalization of the unshakable self-belief that made him the champion he was. To be a winner, he knew that he had to think and talk and act like a winner.

STRATEGIES FOR THINKING YOURSELF TO SUCCESS

Successful athletes often talk about the necessity for a 'positive mental attitude'. To achieve this state, they employ a range of strategies. High on the list is *visualization*. This technique may be adapted by anyone, whatever their area of endeavour, to fit their own individual circumstances:

1. First, formulate a very clear picture of yourself succeeding. Add in lots and lots of detail to make that picture very clear and very real in your mind. To give yourself an idea of how the exercise works, consider the very vivid picture a top-class athlete might paint for himself: Here I am in the starting blocks, oblivious to everything around me. The only thing I can see is that white finishing line 400m away. The only sound I can hear is that of the starting pistol. Bang! And I'm off, barely aware of my own stride and rhythm which, after years of constant practice, is now indelibly imprinted on my muscle memory. I can feel the pain of the lactic acid build up in my muscles, and I'm aware of my limbs growing heavier, but I focus to ignore all that. I keep going, pushing through the pain barrier and suddenly I feel the adrenalin rush and the high of being the first to breast that finishing line. I feel my heart pumping hard and I hear the crowd cheering as someone drapes a Union Jack across my shoulders. I'm too euphoric to feel tired as I dance around on my lap of honour. And now I'm on the podium and I feel the lump in my throat and the surge of pride in my chest as I bow to collect that priceless, shiny gold medal. I can feel the tears pricking in my eyes as I touch it with my fingers and lift it to my lips . . .

The stronger and more detailed the picture you paint, the greater your chance of making it a reality. Once a positive, successful picture is fixed clearly in your mind, any thoughts of failure will find it difficult to intrude. The moment metaphorical rain starts to fall on your pictorial parade, stop the process instantly. Remove all thoughts of *failure* and *defeat* from your mind. The more you consider failure, the more likely the outcome will be failure. The more you concentrate on success, the more likely the outcome will be successful.

2. Next, assess difficulties *realistically*. (Take it from me, this is never best done at three o'clock in the morning.) Always look at problems

objectively in the cold light of day. This helps to ensure that you starve your problems of the mental oxygen of fear. A simple worm of a worry must not be allowed to grow into a python. Once viewed objectively and analytically, most obstacles are far less alarming than we first imagine.

3. Don't imagine for one minute that everyone else has it 'sussed' and that you are the only one obliged to work on your confidence. The world is full of Wizards of Oz, people with more front than Selfridges, who are simply camouflaging their own fundamental lack of confidence. There's nothing wrong with this. If you don't feel genuinely confident, then simply *pretend* that you are.

4. Finally, when you've visualized your positive picture, minimalized your problems, fooled the people until you find you've fooled yourself as well – just leave it alone. *Che sera, sera!*, as the Italians say, '*What will be, will be*' – which, with a postal system like theirs, is the only realistic philosophy. In other words, believe in yourself, do what you can, then quit worrying. Pray to God, if you believe in a Divine Being, or leave it to Fate. Just accept that, once you've done the best you can, all you can do is *trust*.

ACCENTUATE THE POSITIVE, NEUTRALIZE THE NEGATIVE

Certain beliefs, such as religious beliefs, are usually firmly rooted in family background. We are literally born Jewish, Roman Catholic or Muslim. Other beliefs are assimilated along the way. Nigel Wray, a highly successful business and sporting entrepreneur, claims that his own, most helpful beliefs, have been thus acquired: 'I've learned certain beliefs as I've gone along,' he says. 'I now believe in working with people who are enthusiastic and really involved. I'm also convinced of the fundamental merit of sticking at it. Curiously enough, I've often thought that a lack of self-confidence may be the motor that drives people forward. Obviously, you get more confident as you go on but, whatever happens, you must remain aware of the thin line between confidence and arrogance. In any event, I've never allowed a lack of self-confidence to stand in my way. I've just got on with it. It's just one of those things, like my total failure to understand new technology. I find it helps to believe that I'm not alone in my failings, and that they're shared by a few billion others.'

Mike Atherton, the man who has led the England cricket team in more test matches than any other captain, has had more reason than most to contemplate issues of confidence and self-belief. 'I've been helped by my belief in my ability as a player, and by my own confidence in my *mental* capabilities in tough situations. Although I don't have any specific religious beliefs, I do derive great benefit from my constant theological discussions with the Revd Andrew Wingfield Digby, spiritual adviser to the England cricket team! No matter what people say, however, when you're not doing well and you're low on confidence, the self-doubt comes creeping in. Then it's time to consult Bumbles's (David Lloyd's) book on "slump busting"!'

Few people, apart from sports stars and media celebrities, are obliged to conduct their lives under the intense spotlight of media scrutiny. The price of fame and fortune is often an unwelcome dissection of an individual's every strength and weakness. But, whether or not people live their lives under the media glare, their positive, empowering beliefs and their negative, restricting beliefs are often very similar. Take some time to formulate your own positive and empowering beliefs. Consider a few drawn from a wide spectrum of very different individuals who are all, in their own way, winners in the game of life.

POSITIVE, EMPOWERING BELIEFS

You may, along with many others, find strength in the belief of a Divine Being. You may find it helpful to believe in honesty, integrity and the power of listening. What moves you may be either a passionate belief in equality and justice, or a belief in your own strengths and the conviction that you can do it. You may, together with Michael Parkinson, share the positive and empowering belief that 'Yorkshiremen are superior beings' or, with Sir Tim Rice, share a profound belief in 'the Ten Commandments – well, at least some of them'. Michael Cockerell, whose award-winning political documentaries have provided unprecedented insight into, and access to, the nation's major political figures, is consistently motivated by the conviction that 'No' is just an emotional way of saying 'Yes' – a belief which keeps him battling on until his more recalcitrant subjects finally agree to be interviewed.

Your own positive, empowering beliefs might include:

- Everyone can give more if properly motivated and led.
- Success breeds success and *you*, whoever you are, really can make a difference and add value.
- Optimism, confidence in your own ability and the love of a worthwhile challenge will generate success.
- It's up to you to make the most of yourself and your talents: life does not come to you.
- Everyone can change if they want to.
- We are here to improve the world.
- People can always do more than they think they can.

- If you are clear about the outcome and stick to the vision, you will get what you want.
- If you look for the best in people, they will generally respond by delivering it.
- The public good is better than the private gain.
- Competitive practice is always best.
- The value of education and of the arts can never be overestimated.
- A huge enthusiasm for life and living will go a long way towards ensuring personal happiness.
- All people deserve equal opportunities.
- You will get what you want if you want it enough.
- The world is basically unfair and it is our responsibility to make it fairer.
- Whatever happens, everything will be all right, and life is an adventure.
- There is within each of us a god, and walking the talk is magical.
- If someone else can do it, then so can you.
- Anything you can do, I can do better.
- Whatever the prevailing orthodoxy, *my* personal, professional and ethical standards are the right ones.
- The glass is half full, not half empty.
- I am a unique human being, created in the image and likeness of God.

These are the tried and tested beliefs which have enthused, empowered and encouraged people towards their own vision of winning the game of life. Few people, however, have managed to survive fortune's slings and arrows without assimilating at least a few negative beliefs and the doubts and depression which they may engender if left unchecked.

NEGATIVE, DISEMPOWERING BELIEFS

Do you ever find yourself beset by any of these negative, disempowering beliefs?

- I am not good enough.
- I'm worried that I sound inarticulate and that I'm not good on my feet.
- I'm never going to manage to pull this off.
- I can't do that.
- There's no point even trying for the job. Women will always be discriminated against in favour of men.
- I'm not as clever, good-looking and well connected as other people.
- Surely it wasn't really me who achieved that. It must have been luck.
- I'm not feeling 100 per cent confident right now and therefore I won't succeed.
- The scenario is changing and it's bound to be for the worse.

You may identify with some of these, or you may have your own private collection of negative niggles. Few people meet the challenge of perennial optimism. Everyone of insight has the occasional long, dark night of the soul. The key, however, is to find your own way of arresting those negative beliefs before they create serious doubt and depression.

'Feeling down? Buy a hat!' – from childhood, I recall this fail-safe recipe as advocated by my home town department store. The magic of millinery always struck me as a dubious anti-depressant but, judging by the magnificent confections sported every Sunday at our local church, the pink chiffon pill-box must have been the Prozac of the 1960s. A hat, a hymn or a holiday – whatever it may be, decide on your own strategy for over-riding negative thoughts and beliefs. In the next section, I shall outline a few 'slump-busting' suggestions you may find helpful.

STRATEGIES FOR COPING WITH NEGATIVE BELIEFS

- You must recognize that energy is a precious resource, so please don't waste it by worrying.
- It's important to factor enough leisure time into your life. When things feel as if they're getting you down – try taking an away day.
- Whenever you're feeling down, or that you may be falling short of the mark, remind yourself of all the things you've achieved and done well. Don't stint yourself. Think of everything – even that badge for good deportment you won in the Third Form. Once you've done your 'success' tally, you'll be able to put your current doubts or misgivings into their proper perspective.
- Some people say you learn from experience, but that's not strictly true. You only learn from experience if you're wise enough to analyse it and understand what happened, and why. If ever you're feeling low, figure out the reasons why and deal with them. If you've made mistakes, learn from them and resolve not to repeat them. Nothing is more depressing and, ultimately, more debilitating, than making the same mistake again and again. If you fail to learn from your own mistakes, it's easy to start believing that there's no way you can exercise control in your life.
- When you feel the gloom creeping in, do something you really love or at which you excel. It doesn't much matter what it is – the great British statesman, Sir Winston Churchill, used to go out and build walls. If you completely immerse yourself in something, you'll often find the black

cloud disappears while you're not watching. The point is that success in anything will serve to reaffirm self-confidence.

■ To counteract negativity, start believing all the good things people say about you. If you allow it, external verification will build up your confidence. When you find that others really rate you, you tend to live up to their expectations. In good schools, companies and organizations, people feel 'rated'. When you don't feel valued or rated, there's a terrible temptation to 'live down' to expectations and to under-perform. Make sure you feel you're valued.

■ Even if you're not feeling confident, act as if you are! Remember to fake it till you make it, and the *more* you practise, the *luckier* you'll get!

■ Talk yourself up and then wise yourself up. Enthusiasm and encouragement are your greatest allies.

■ Discuss your negative feelings and thoughts with others. It helps to talk, but once you've got them off your chest, move forward.

■ Remember that the worst case scenario that you spent all night worrying about *will probably never happen.*

■ Persistence is the key to circumventing all obstacles, material or mental. If at first you don't succeed, try, try again.

BELIEF EQUALS HAPPINESS EQUALS PERSONAL FULFILMENT

> Most people are as happy as they decide to be.
>
> Abraham Lincoln

Objective fact cannot hold a candle to subjective reality. You are what you believe. If the poorest beggar in Calcutta *decides* to feel happy, then that's exactly what he is. Conversely, if the most gifted, loving, kind and attractive person on the face of the earth *decides* to feel miserable, then that's what she is. Whatever images clever advertisers may employ to project the concept of wellbeing and enjoyment (boobs, booze or Bisto – surely the ideal commercial should involve an amalgam of all three), nothing can really make us happy except our own decision to be so and our own belief that we are. Control over our own feelings is the greatest power of all. If you can elect how you are going to feel or react in any given situation, you will have managed to achieve complete self-mastery.

Adversity cannot upset you if you *refuse* to allow it. Unhappiness is a choice: you are as happy as you choose to be.

> It's up to *you* whether you feel over the moon, or sick as the proverbial parrot.

All it takes to move from one state to another is a change in your perception. Attitude is more important than fact and, with practice, you can learn how to control your own mental attitude. The trauma of an unexpected job loss can be transformed into an exciting opportunity to explore new possibilities, to become self-employed or to set up your own business. The hassle of finding yourself obliged to move from your much-loved neck of the woods to another part of the country may be offset by the joy of recalling the net-twitching nosiness of your current ghastly neighbours. Even the adversity of accident or illness can be used to positive effect. In such instances, tremendous courage is required not to slip into all-too understandable self-pity. However, by concentrating on all the positive aspects of what is inevitable, as opposed to what ideally *might have been*, it becomes easier to adopt a more positive and hopeful attitude.

What we believe, how we feel, and the way we think all have a definite impact on our physical wellbeing. Think about the times you've been bored – how swiftly mental fatigue swiftly sets in and how quickly the body follows suit. By contrast, think of how you feel when you're truly enjoying yourself – somehow you seem to have endless reserves of energy and the hours pass by unnoticed. Hard physical work may exhaust you, but, however strenuous, it will never sap your energy in the same destructive fashion as the drain of emotional upheaval.

Much of the emotional upheaval we experience is due to 'slippage' in our lives, that's to say the dislocation between what we *want* to happen and what is *actually* happening. This may be a difference between the way we want to be, live, or look, and the way we actually are – or it may be something far more corrosive. The most serious 'slippage' of all occurs when there is a distinct lack of congruency between what we *believe* and how we *behave*. If, for example, you believe in honesty and integrity, you'll find it difficult (possibly even depressing) to work in an environment where the people around you are crooked. If understanding, care and compassion are important to you, you'll find it impossible to tolerate gross acts of selfishness and insensitivity committed by others around you. In such situations, biting the proverbial lip amounts to tacit acceptance and, if we consistently fail to react, we begin to despise ourselves. Our actions are at odds with our beliefs and nothing is more emotionally destructive. In such situations, you have only two options: either work to change the environment around you or get out of it as quickly as possible. Whatever you're doing, *always believe in what you do and do what you believe.* For your own physical, mental and emotional wellbeing, be sure to walk your talk.

CHAPTER ELEVEN

the art of captaincy

The final test of a leader is that he leaves behind him in other men the conviction and the will to carry on. The genius of a good leader is to leave behind him a situation which common sense, without the grace of genius, can deal with successfully.

From *Roosevelt Has Gone*, Walter Lippman

A leader is best when people barely know he exists, not so good when people obey and acclaim him. Worst when they despise him.

Fail to honour the people –
And they'll fail to honour you.

> But of a good leader, who talks little,
> When his work is done, his aim fulfilled,
> They will all say:
> 'We did this ourselves.'
>
> Lao-Tzu

What constitutes a good leader? Is it the ambitious individual who has clambered to the top of the greasy pole of politics? The chief executive officer running a successful multimillion-pound corporation? The groundbreaking scientist whose discoveries have transformed our daily lives? Or is it the penniless spiritual leader whose convictions and behaviour imbue us with a belief in something greater than ourselves?

The qualities of good leadership may be present in these individuals, but they may also be found in many far more anonymous, and yet no less 'successful', individuals. A financially struggling single parent who manages to bring up balanced, loving and socially responsible children may well display more genuine leadership characteristics than all of the nation's politicians put together. In the same way, a beleaguered headmistress determined to turn around a struggling inner city 'sink' school will need to call upon just as many leadership skills as any FTSE 100 chief executive. Leadership may involve a country, a company, a community, a school, a team, a family or it may involve no one other than *you*.

Whatever you're doing and however you're involved, you're constantly being required to demonstrate your own leadership qualities. You, after all, are confronting the greatest leadership challenge of them all. You're the captain and you're playing to win the game of your life.

Throughout history, successful leaders have often been associated with qualities such as physical courage, aggressiveness, boldness, vision and decisiveness. In the days of pitched battle, such characteristics were rightly prized. The name of Alexander the Great, King of Macedon in the first century BC, is synonymous with such traditionally masculine leadership qualities. History books revel in the details of his magnificent campaigns; his dream to unite the Greek race in a war against the all-powerful Persian empire; his enormous personal courage and boundless energy; his capacity for brilliantly daring strategic thinking.

Whatever classical history books may focus on, however, the qualities which made Alexander the truly great leader he indubitably was, were, above all, his charisma, understanding, compassion and empathy. True, he could be cruel and perfidious and, towards the end, like so many leaders, he succumbed to vainglory and megalomania. But for most of his extraordinary life and military career, his real genius lay in his ability to motivate others to achieve the apparently impossible.

Alexander believed in leading by example and his energy was legendary. At night, after long marches, he would refuse to rest until he had wandered around the camp to talk and, more important still, to *listen* to his soldiers. His empathy and concern were so obviously genuine that men followed him, not out of fear, but out of *love and respect*. Alexander encouraged everyone to share his dream, and he made them feel part of his overall plan. Every individual felt intimately involved. Equally important, he demonstrated by his actions that there was nothing he would ask of his men which he was not prepared to do himself.

Nowadays, 'Emotional Intelligence' is discussed as if it were a revolutionary new concept in leadership but, even while he was on a campaign, Alexander (a quintessential 'Boys Own' hero) understood the basic good leadership principles of caring, communicating and making the people around him feel valued. Although at first glance not the most obvious candidate, Alexander did exhibit many of the intuitive leadership qualities which today have taken on such fancy labels as Emotional Intelligence, or

'Sensitivity Quotient'. However current business gurus care to dress it up, your grandmother, my grandmother and even Alexander the Great's grand-mother would have known that all we're really talking about is good old common sense.

The art of leadership has spawned thousands of training programmes, but there's no reason to shroud the whole business of leadership in mystique. Reduced to its simplest terms, leadership is simply a matter of horses for courses. Different times, environments and situations require different types of leaders and different leadership qualities. Even Alexander might struggle as a modern-day United Nations Secretary-General although, on the plus side, talk-time would be mercifully truncated. In the same way, the bold, aggressive entrepreneur whose forceful personality has created a thriving company from the ether may not possess the requisite skills to manage the subsequent stages of the company's development. 'Horses for courses, plus common sense' or, to append an impressively meaningless business guru acronym, 'HoCoCoS'™ (Trade mark: Frances Edmonds) – when it's stripped to the bone, that's all there is to leadership.

There is, however, one catch in this deceptively simple leadership lark. The 'Horses for courses plus common sense' requirements keep changing, particularly the 'Horses for courses' element. 'Traditional' leadership quali-ties which may have worked well in the past may not be sufficient for sur-vival in the future. In the working environment, the classic Big Boss bullying techniques such as 'Divide and rule', 'Rule by fear', 'Do it my way' or even so-called 'Creative Tension' (the strategy of creating a stressful environment where everyone feels insecure about his job or prospects, and is thus con-stantly kept on his toes) are no longer perceived by everyone as signs of good leadership.

> You do not lead people by hitting them over the head. That's assault, not leadership.
>
> *Dwight D. Eisenhower*

A cursory glance at the nation's boardrooms, areas still dominated by white, middle-aged, middle-class men, would suggest that general thinking on leadership has not changed radically since the Victorian era. Whatever hymns we hear lifted in praise of sensitivity, empathy and communication, the strong but hard, inspiring but arrogant leader does not yet feature on the endangered species list. But his days are numbered. All over the world, the movement towards increased diversity in the workforce means that we no longer think it extraordinary for women to work side by side with men, for blacks to work with whites, Catholics with Protestants. The challenge of managing this rich and multi-faceted diversity requires a new kind of leader, just as the challenge of creating effective teams from the wealth of different talents, backgrounds and perspectives which such diversity creates demands different leadership characteristics. It's always possible, if you're prepared to pay the price, to buy a man's time and physical presence. Time and physical presence alone, however, will never generate success in any area. Real success is rooted in loyalty and devotion. In companies, as in families, these responses can never be demanded, only earned.

In society and at work, the traditional, rigidly structured hierarchy is also on the slippery slope. Although meritocracy has yet to infiltrate certain well-defended bastions of the British Establishment, talent is increasingly more valued than title. An additional phenomenon is also reshaping the way we think about the structure of any given organization and the status of the individual within it. The explosion of information technology now means that employees who were historically on the bottom rung of the corporation are now more important than ever. Where the consumer is king, customer service is often the added value element which determines the choices the consumer will make. The airline booking clerk on the other end of the phone, the department store assistant, the individual manning the helpline when your computer system jams – these are increasingly the people who make the all-important *impression*. Far more than any anonymous boardroom suit, these 'bottom-rung' folk are the ones who represent the company and who define its image in the eyes of the consumer.

> A corporation that successfully draws on the talents and abilities of all its employees as individuals will be the best positioned for success.
>
> *James R. Houghton – Coming*

The idea that the general direction of an organization will somehow filter down from a remote and autocratic 'top' has reached its sell-by date. In the future, direction is far more likely to come directly from the customer/consumer up. The businesses which will survive and thrive are therefore those which can respond to the customers' needs swiftly and efficiently. The ability to produce this rapid response requires, in turn, the effort of the whole team functioning effectively together, not the built-in divisiveness of the rigidly stratified hierarchy of yesteryear. More than ever before, flexibility, adaptability and teamwork will determine who has the competitive edge in the future.

> The winners in the future will be those who can develop a culture that allows them to move faster, communicate more clearly, and involve everyone in a focused effort to serve ever more demanding customers.
>
> *John F. Welch Jr. – General Electric*

In the corporate environment, the increased penetration of electronic communication has delivered Marshall McLuhan's prophecy of the Global Village. Instant communication via the Internet has transformed the way people do business. Markets, nowadays, are global. Thanks to the worldwide web, an amateur market gardener growing bonzai trees in the Highlands and islands of Scotland can land a multimillion-pound contract from a Japanese interior designer in Tokyo – and all this thanks to her techie teenage son who spent his half-term creating a website for her. More than ever before, the world is an 'on-liner's oyster'. Highly diversified global markets demand something other than traditional leadership qualities. In such a rapidly fluctuating environment, the unexpected must always be expected. Successful leaders know how to keep ahead of the game and how, simultaneously, to direct it. Truly visionary leaders go even further. In the game of life, winners go out and create their own game.

Moving outside the workplace, we can't help noticing that the family and family life reflect similarly monumental shifts. Women's educational and financial emancipation has put paid to the quintessentially hypocritical Victorian paradigm of 'happy' family life. Neither women nor children are now regarded as chattels to be patronized and protected (at best) or bossed and beaten (at worst). In families which function successfully, every individual is valued and treated with respect. Within the security of such an environment, the individual swiftly learns his rights, his responsibilities and his boundaries. He knows he can expect support and is equally happy to lend it. A successful family (which in no way suggests any so-called 'pre-ferred model') is one which functions as a team in which everyone under-stands the role he or she must play. The role of the parent (team leader) is to encourage everyone within the family (team) to play their part as well as possible and to lend support along the way. Nowadays, the good parent and the good chief executive officer must learn to function alike.

> Controlling monsters have given way to coaching mentors.

Clarity and communication, support and solidarity – successful indivi-duals, families, teams and companies demonstrate many of the same characteristics.

THE ESSENTIAL QUALITIES OF GOOD LEADERSHIP – THE HORSES FOR COURSES THEORY

Leadership skills differ according to the time, the place and the task. Even in a horses for courses situation, however, every horse should meet the basic four-leg requirement. In much the same way, good leadership involves cer-tain key attributes whatever the situation. Add to those the ultimate magic ingredients of charisma, compassion and empathy, and the good leader becomes truly great.

Team sport provides endless examples of inspirational leadership, all the more so because the results of sporting endeavour are unequivocal and immediately obvious. Cliff Morgan, the much loved Welsh rugby international who went on to run the Outside Broadcasting Group for BBC television, underscores the essential leadership qualities of generosity, focus, courage and intelligence: 'A good leader has the ability to identify talent and develop it,' he says. 'He must have the stature to accept responsibility through good times and bad and also have the courage to make difficult decisions. He must be able to inspire and encourage others more than they would have believed possible. In addition, he must keep a clear and precise idea of objectives and be able to communicate effectively.'

David Ross, co-founder of Carphone Warehouse and a 1990s retailing phenomenon, believes that leadership is based on vision which, in turn, implies foresight in spotting gaps in the market. In the mid 1980s he and his partner Chris Dunstone identified the problems which the average man in the street (the plumber, the market stall holder, the builder – i.e. precisely the sort of bloke who needed a mobile phone) encountered when trying to purchase one. In those days, corporate buyers were the name of the game and potential individual purchasers and their requirements were simply ignored. For this wider, more disparate public, Ross and Dunstone realized that there were no places in which the individuals could browse and ask which mobile phones and tariff deals were available. Spotting this huge gap in the market, the two friends soon developed a vision of selling mobile phones from high street shops and they duly kicked off with their first retailing site just off London's Marylebone Road. Carphone Warehouse was born and, funding their growth with cash-flow, continued to expand.

In David Ross's view, *focus* is an equally important skill in leadership. In the case of Carphone Warehouse, focus means a single-minded approach to customers and their ever-developing needs. Good leadership also demands a passion for the business and an innate understanding of what the customer really wants. 'Most important of all,' says David, 'leadership demands *ruthless* delegation. You've got to understand that you haven't got time to do everything and you mustn't feel guilty about that. Your task is to keep your mind focused on the bigger picture – the vision – and that, in turn, involves an ability to choose good, trustworthy people to whom you can delegate.'

The leadership qualities individuals most value are often determined by their own careers and background. The career of Sir Victor Blank has spanned three distinct phases. At the extraordinarily young age of twenty-seven, Sir Victor was made a partner at Clifford Turner (now Clifford Chance), the City's premier law firm, where he ran the firm's mergers and acquisitions business. In 1981, he was offered the chance to become head of corporate finance at Charterhouse, then a struggling merchant bank which he, as chairman, transformed into one of the best known firms in the City. From there, he moved into his third corporate career which involves, amongst other things, the chairmanship of Trinity Mirror Group and Great Universal Stores. 'In politics, Nelson Mandela is a classic example of a man who never allowed either his vision or his judgement to be impaired, as it so easily could have been, by bitterness and rancour,' he observes. 'Judgement must never be clouded by emotion – that's a key leadership issue.'

Vision, focus, discipline, determination – the words recur constantly in the lexicons of leadership. Sporting and business entrepreneur Nigel Wray who, amongst other interests, controls Saracens Rugby Club, also points to people skills and 'stickability'. 'To be a good leader in any area, it's crucial to know how to get on with people,' he believes. 'Good leaders also know how to make decisions and then how to implement them. After that, they have the guts to stick with whatever decision has been taken.'

Whether you're a struggling single mum or captain of the All Blacks, it's up to you to inspire, motivate, enthuse and generally get the best out of the others around you. To do this, you'll have to get your message across by communicating clearly. More important still, you'll have to demonstrate that amalgam of compassion and resolution often referred to as 'tough love'. In both instances, the individuals concerned face the same continuous, uphill struggle. Both, in their own ways, are required to show leadership. The only difference is that the 'Children Challenge' is never crowned with public recognition or awards (except, perhaps, the greatest reward of all).

Good leaders must have a clear vision and good communication skills. Frequently forgotten, however (often by our politicians, and always at their peril), is that communication involves the ability to *listen* as well as the ability to *explain*. As every good parent knows, talking *at* children is a complete waste of time. Children will only listen to you if they know that you, in turn, are prepared to listen to them. Whatever the area, leaders need both the *internal* skill of developing a vision and the *external* skill of being able to communicate that vision if they are to be truly effective. A parent, captain or chief executive with ideas and goals he is unable to articulate is unlikely to be able to direct his 'team' towards that vision. Without the necessary communication skills, there is no team lingua franca, no shared language which ensures that everyone involved is clear about what the team goals, tactics, strategy and philosophy actually are.

Leadership involves taking control. Whether you want to take control of your own destiny (I want to change jobs, become fit, get out of this no-hope relationship) or that of an entire organization (I want to make this company the recognized market leader), you must be clear about where you are now, where you're going next, and how you're going to get there. In one celebrated passage in Lewis Carroll's wonderful book, *Alice in Wonderland*, the lost and confused Alice reaches a crossroads and, unable to make up her mind which way to take, stops to ask the grinning Cheshire Cat for directions. The cat, in turn, asks Alice where precisely she wants to go, to which

Alice replies that she really doesn't know. The cat is unimpressed. If Alice doesn't know where she wants to go, he observes, then it doesn't much matter which road she takes!

The same Cheshire Cat logic holds true for individuals and organizations everywhere. How can anyone know which metaphorical map to unfold if the destination has not yet been identified? How can anyone determine the best route or strategy when no one even knows where the route or strategy is leading? If you know where you're going then, even it involves a few unforeseen dead ends and detours, the chances are you'll get there in the end . If you don't know where you are to start with, the chances are you'll end up going nowhere.

A person leading his own life must be able to define his ultimate destination. If, in addition, he is entrusted with the task of leading others, he must be able to communicate that destination clearly to those around him. This does not imply that he must feel obliged to direct or issue directions to his team every inch of the way towards the final objective. The 'traditional' boss of yesteryear was often excessively hands-on: things had to be done in a certain way and that was, inevitably, *my way*. Such an authoritarian, directive style is often seen to come a cropper when the proverbial cat is away. Modern, effective leaders understand the need to allow individuals the freedom, authority and, thereby, the responsibility to function autonomously. In the work environment, the effective leader will ensure that everyone has the optimum conditions to function effectively (the right tools, the necessary information, a clear view of what is expected, a healthy environment etc.). He then empowers the members of his team by allowing them to get on with the job as best they know how. At home, the team captain parent will do her/his best to create a loving, stable and secure environment from which each of the team players (children and spouse) will draw the confidence to develop and achieve.

The curious paradox of empowerment is that, in order to gain power, power must be given away. The more individuals are empowered, however, the more they need strategic thinkers at the helm – leaders with the vision to set the goals and determine which way that particular operation is going. There's nothing more demotivating than over-direction and even small children abreact to the indignity of being constantly checked and monitored. In the family and in the workplace, optimum arrangements are based on mutual trust, respect and the understanding that each individual will do his best to fulfil agreed expectations. Within the context of certain well-defined objectives, members of the family, team or organization must be allowed the freedom to do their own thing. Good leaders recognize the need for this autonomy. They understand the importance of being able to delegate or 'let go'. By letting go, a good leader can free himself up to get on with *his* job, which is communicating objectives so that they're clearly understood, ensuring the commitment of all concerned to reaching those objectives, and creating the impetus to get things done.

Good leaders do not boss, bully or babysit (except, of course, in the literal sense). The leader who not only develops and communicates the vision, but also goes out and *lives* it will not be merely good, but also positively inspirational. In their ancient wisdom, the American Red Indians used to believe that to explain something to someone was, in effect, to steal from them because it deprived them of the opportunity for learning. Great leaders function in much the same way as great parents and great teachers. They understand that the lessons they allow us to learn for ourselves are the lessons we'll always remember. Indeed, it is a truth almost universally disregarded that the classroom has much to teach the boardroom in terms of 'employee' empowerment. No nursery school teacher worthy of the name would even dream of telling children that, say, salt is soluble and sand is insoluble. Those measuring jugs would be out, puddles of water would be on the floor, and mixtures of salt and sand caked all over everyone's clothes but, at the end of the day, the children would know (and remember for ever) because they had seen it for themselves – that salt dissolves in water and sand does not.

Good teachers are adept at the key communication skill of 'show, not tell'. In addition, like all great leaders, they demonstrate something far more rare and precious even than outstanding ability: *they possess the ability to recognize ability.* They are adept at spotting and nurturing talent in others; they understand that the surest way to draw out and develop the best in other people is by genuine appreciation and encouragement. A great teacher will not stop until she has located that vein of gold present within every child, that talent which, once recognized and tapped, will help the child fulfil his true potential. In the same way, a great captain knows how to meld the vast array of differing talents present in any team into a cohesive unit while, at the same time, satisfying the demands of the most demanding folk on earth – the fans! A few decent school ma'ams in British boardrooms, and this country would again rule the world! Good parents, teachers, captains and leaders don't spend their time catching things going wrong. Instead, they strive to create an environment in which the people around them are inspired to develop, thrive and succeed.

One of the most destructive feelings any child can experience is that of injustice. However old we are, the intensity of that emotion never leaves us and the belief that 'It's not fair' – whether real or perceived – remains as corrosive in adults as it is in children. A good leader, if he is to inspire respect, must demonstrate a relentless passion for justice. Moral fervour, however, must never be confused with pious proselytizing. Good leaders know that actions speak louder than words and that, in order to convince people, they must consistently walk the talk. It is not, after all, what you preach but how you behave that counts and, in the media-intrusive world which we inhabit, the 'do-as-I-say-but-not-as-I-do philosophy' is rarely a sustainable option. Good leaders are straight dealers who demonstrate consistent honesty and integrity.

Another key leadership skill is an ability to understand and respect what another person is feeling. Good leaders empathize with other people. While taking on board other people's problems, however, a good leader will try to remain enthusiastic. Even in the face of adversity, he or she will always endeavour to put that best foot forward. In the event of success, a good leader refuses to be fazed and never rests on the proverbial laurels. He or she knows that complacency is the mother of mediocrity and mediocrity, in turn, is the father of failure.

Mike Brearley, arguably England's most successful cricket captain ever, was deservedly celebrated for his capacity to get the very best out of his players. His book, *The Art of Captaincy*, widely regarded as a classic of its type, describes the man-management skills he employed to direct and motivate characters as diverse and, on occasion, as difficult, as Geoffrey Boycott and Ian Botham. As a deep thinker of the game of cricket, and human behaviour generally (he now practises as a professional psycho-therapist), Brearley underlines the need for constant interaction between the captain of any team and his players. In addition, he emphasizes the need for a leader to know how to sort out good advice from bad, and also to have the ability to know when, and when not, to seek advice. A good captain must also know how to cope with a multitude of conflicting demands and at the same time pay attention to the different roles which individuals may be expected, and must be encouraged, to play within a team. 'Above all,' Brearley says, 'the most admirable leadership qualities are a capacity to listen and a capacity to tell. Add to these courage, creativity and humility and you have a truly great leader.'

Another highly successful England cricket captain, Mike Atherton, is a single-minded battler of immense determination. Atherton has always been a cricketer more intent on improving his game and motivating his men than accommodating the fourth estate with glib quotations. Sports journalists do not warm to people who do not fill their copy, and Atherton has come in for more than his fair share of adverse media comment. Cussed, awkward, stubborn, determined – these are the epithets most regularly applied to Mike Atherton and yet these are the very qualities which made him the cricketer and the leader he became. Cricket lovers all over the world will recall his extraordinarily gritty innings of 185 to save the test match for England against South Africa in Johannesburg during the 1995/96 series. And a similarly gutsy performance against Pakistan in December, 2000. A combination of determination, confidence – and perhaps the burning desire to prove his critics wrong – these have been the hallmarks of Atherton's career. 'As a good leader,' he says, 'you must have confidence, enthusiasm, faith in your players, an optimistic outlook and, most important of all, you must have the respect of the team as a player, leader and human being. The crucial art of leadership is the ability to stay calm under pressure and still have the guts to gamble when the pressure is on rather than retreat into a shell.'

One woman not naturally given to shell-seeking, and the only England cricket captain never to have lost a test match, is Rachael Heyhoe-Flint. An indomitable lady, full of zest and fun, Rachael spearheaded a vigorous campaign for women's right of entry to the male-only preserve of the Marylebone Cricket Club. For those who know her, the outcome of the Flintstone v. Buffers-in-Blazers contest was never in doubt, and Rachael duly assumed her rightful place as one of the first female members of one of the nation's last all-male bastions. 'To be a good leader,' she emphasizes, 'you must demonstrate enthusiasm, efficiency and the ability to communicate. Apart from that, you must only ask people to do what you know you yourself are capable of doing.'

Empathy, Ethics and Enthusiasm – the three Es – good leaders all demonstrate these qualities. In addition, a great leader will generally have keen intelligence coupled with solid common sense and will not usually be hampered by an enormous ego. Self-centred people with overly developed egos rarely make good leaders as they often lack the insight and generosity to give others the credit or support they need. Good leaders must also be able to make and take quick decisions and maintain that all-important balance in their lives. Vision, integrity, drive, energy, a sense of purpose and the gift of motivating others by 'telling the story' – these are key leadership attributes. Equally important, a good leader must have a clear understanding of the people around him, his environment and culture. Most important of all, however, a good leader must be courageous enough to think for himself and lucky enough to exhibit perfect timing.

As Louis Pasteur once observed, 'Chance favours the prepared mind.' However you care to define luck, Archie Norman, the entrepreneur who turned around the fortunes of the ailing supermarket chain ASDA, possesses it in spades. Every business venture he touches seems destined to turn to gold. In his first six years as ASDA's chief executive, investors in the company saw a 600 per cent return on their money. His next challenge, to drag a roundly beaten Conservative party kicking and screaming into the twenty-first century, proved somewhat more problematic, but he set about modernizing Conservative Party Central Office with the reforming zeal of a missionary. A free thinker who believes that the worst thing any chief executive can do is to sit behind a large, self-aggrandizing desk in a large piece of prime space, he has never been afraid of attacking sacred corporate cows. 'It's the ability to focus that makes a good leader,' says Archie Norman, 'and also the courage to lead from the front. Great leaders know how to touch people directly and how to draw in good advice. They must also demonstrate relentless energy. Stamina is essential.'

Tim Waterstone, whose high-street bookstores transformed literary Britain, is a man who, by his own admission, 'likes to attack life'. At the same time, he underscores the essential human ingredient of good leadership: 'Clarity of purpose and humanity in its application,' says Tim Waterstone. 'These, together with courage, plus ethical and moral steadfastness, are the true qualities of leadership.'

SO WHO SHOULD BE CAPTAIN?

Good leaders are people who are *prepared to listen* to others, and value their opinions, but who are *not deterred* from pursuing their own firmly held beliefs or goals. Leaders in life are conciliators, adept at conflict management, but they are not afraid of being unpopular in the pursuit of their ideals. Every good leader believes strongly in his goal or mission and is able to communicate a vision which has practical application to the here and now. Good leaders must be both strategic planners *and* risk takers. They do not back down at the first sign of adversity, but they must have the intelligence to see and admit when they are wrong. The great leader must remain approachable and willing and eager to learn. He or she must also, ideally, exhibit tact, charm, humility and a capacity to forgive. The good leader finds time to listen, then knows how to delegate.

A tall order? Let's take a look at the skills required to take your team and yourself to the top.

CHAPTER TWELVE

leading from the front

The very essence of leadership is that you have to have a vision.
It's got to be a vision you articulate clearly and forcefully on
every occasion. You can't blow an uncertain trumpet.

Father T. Hesburgh

THE NINE KEY LEADERSHIP QUALITIES

1. Self-knowledge or sense of self
2. Vision – creativity – imagination
3. Integrity

4. Courage
5. Responsibility and responsiveness
6. Belief in people – team building
7. Passion and enthusiasm
8. Energy – positive demeanour
9. Communication skills

Self-knowledge or Sense of Self

> To thine own self be true, and it must follow, as the night the
> day, thou canst not then be false to any man.
>
> *Hamlet*, I.iii

Whether you're leading your own life or leading other people, success depends on *understanding and believing in yourself.* Feel good about yourself. Whoever you are, you're a unique and special blend of talents. Kick off by giving yourself a cheer for all your many good points. High self-esteem and strong self-image have nothing whatsoever to do with arrogance or self-regard. Just take a look at leaders of the stature of Gandhi in his simple loin cloth, or Mother Teresa, whose only personal possessions were her sari and her cooking pot, and understand how high self-esteem may co-exist quite happily with humility. When you're feeling good about yourself, you're 'centred' and you exude an air of quiet self-confidence. As the French would say, you feel good in your skin. So take time to understand what moves you, motivates you and generally makes you tick. Let's face it, if you don't understand what makes *you* tick, how can you possibly understand what's driving anyone else? Be honest with yourself and realistic about your own strengths and weaknesses. Honesty begets trust, trust begets loyalty, and loyalty creates healthy relationships which form the basis of successful families, teams and businesses.

> You are searching for the magic key that will unlock the door to the source of power: and yet you have the key in your own hands.
>
> *Napoleon Hill*
>
> True power resides in knowing yourself.

Vision – Creativity – Imagination

> Vision without action is merely a dream. Action without vision is just passing the time. Vision with action can change the world.
>
> Joel Barker

Great leaders, such as Dr Martin Luther King and Nelson Mandela, had dreams so compelling that they were prepared to die for them. Few visions demand the ultimate sacrifice, but all involve hard work and commitment in their implementation. Leaders constantly demonstrate creativity and imagination in painting their powerful pictures for other people. With his deeply moving 'I have a dream' speech, Dr Martin Luther King managed to galvanize an entire nation. His powerful oratorical skills – the lyricism, the cadences and the flow of his words – combined to reinforce his vision of an American nation united in freedom, peace and brotherhood.

But the vision, imagination and creativity which are necessary to lead others may be demonstrated in many other less obvious ways. Some great leaders and opinion formers manage to persuade, not so much by their communication skills, but simply by their actions. Mother Teresa never displayed any great oratorical skills, but her obvious devotion to the poor and hopeless of Calcutta was a far more eloquent testament to her commitment than anything she might ever have said.

Integrity

If you're not honest by nature, so the old French saying goes, be honest out of self-interest. In the end, dishonesty is always rumbled. In other words, you can't fool all of the people all of the time.

In the corporate world, integrity has often been considered a disposable luxury. Fund your right-on marketing campaign in the West with sweat-shop labour in the East. In today's world of increased consumer awareness, however, an unwavering commitment to values is justifiably prized. The Body Shop's Anita Roddick founded her business on a commitment to sell only beauty products made without animal testing. She was prepared to walk her talk and, having hit a public nerve, created a successful and much emulated business. A firm commitment to principles pays dividends both in public and private life.

Courage

> Courage is contagious. If a brave man takes a stand, the spines
> of others are stiffened.
>
> Billy Graham

Few of us are 'martyr material', i.e., prepared to lay down our lives for our beliefs, and yet most of us are required to exhibit considerable reserves of courage in our everyday dealings. You may, for example, take a stand by refusing to ignore racist or sexist comments on the football terraces: you may set your face against the bully in the office or the playground. Perhaps you may agree to implement an unpopular, but necessary, policy at work or demonstrate the intellectual rigour to contradict the prevailing orthodoxy within your community. All these are stands which demand guts, determination and strength of purpose.

Courage comes in many forms, from the life-saving bravery of the fireman to the gut-wrenching agonies experienced by the nursery school's carol concert soloist. Often, however, it is the very process of making the decision to do something which requires the greatest courage of all. Implicit in decision-making is the possibility of getting it wrong. It is precisely this fear of making a mistake that has been known to paralyse even the most able of people.

> The greatest risk in life is the risk of doing
> nothing at all.
>
> *Sir Martin Sorrell, Chief Executive WPP*

A good general, as Napoleon once said, is a general who makes decisions. The ability to make a decision, allied to the courage to carry it through, is crucial to effective leadership.

'To make any decision,' advises Sir Victor Blank, 'you must gather the relevant information, analyse it, assess the risk, then decide. Information, analysis, risk-assessment, decision – in theory, it's as simple as that. Once the decision is made, then do whatever needs to be done and be prepared to live with the consequences. You must understand that, whatever happens, there's no point looking back.'

The same decision-making technique holds true in personal as well as in professional life. In personal relationships, no one likes to be 'kept dangling'. Children, in particular, hate uncertainty. Indeed, whatever the situation, we all prefer to know where we stand. Just like muscles in the body, our decision-making 'muscles' will atrophy unless they are constantly in use. In business, the ability to respond by making swift decisions is often the difference between success and failure. On a more personal and individual level, the pressure of problems which remain unresolved, and decisions which remain untaken, are the root of much stress and depression. People often find that the very fact of making a decision, whatever the decision, will release the mental log-jam and improve the situation. A decision made usually implies a goal, something to work towards (even if what you're working towards is the fact of 'putting something behind you'), a process which in itself is constructive.

Decision-making is rarely simple and everyone knows how exhausting the 'on the one hand' and 'on the other hand' routine can be. The classic list of pros and cons will stretch to eternity if allowed. Save yourself time and heartache by learning to cut to the chase. Put in place your own subconscious decision-making technique. Whatever the issue, resolve to gather the information, complete the analysis, consider the possible upside and downside, make the decision, study the outcome and then, most important, move on. Whatever happens, don't waste hours of your time in pointless hand-wringing when there's already another pressing decision waiting in the wings.

> Assess what needs to be done. Set priorities and deadlines. Then get on with it!

Responsibility and Responsiveness

> When things go wrong, a leader says, '*I am responsible.*' When things go reasonably well, the leader says, '*We did it!*' When things go very well, the leader says, '*They did it.*'
>
> Dr Michael LeBoeuf

> No problem is so big and complicated that it can't be run away from.
>
> Charlie Brown

One of the clearest signs of maturity and integrity in any individual and, even more so, of any leader is the willingness to accept responsibility for the decisions he or she might make. This may prove a difficult burden to bear, especially when the decision in question is the product of consensus and other parties are involved. The buck, however, must always stop with the top dog. Responsibility goes with the rations of leadership, and you'll find the load less onerous to bear if you first gain a clear grasp of all the details involved in any difficult decision. First-hand familiarity with the facts, not a second-hand acceptance of the regurgitated issues, will not only make for a better decision, but also for greater *ownership* of that decision once it has been made.

A good leader will place great emphasis on information, analysis and consultation. Whether you're responsible for your own wellbeing or that of a family, team, company or country, it's up to you to assimilate and analyse the information and to make the final tough decisions. You can always leave the easy decisions aside, and take them later. In families, for instance, parents often allow their children confidence-building autonomy in minor issues (e.g., which snack or breakfast cereal they'd prefer to eat), while retaining authority over the bigger questions (where the family lives, which schools the children attend etc.). Difficult decisions require the essential leadership skill of vision and, in taking those tough decisions, you must retain the ability to focus on long-term goals and also the discipline to avoid being sidetracked by the minutiae of inevitable, everyday dilemmas.

Decision-making is an art, not a science, so don't be afraid to listen to your gut feeling. When you're in touch with your emotions and when you use those emotions to fine-tune your intuition, then you're far more likely to be able to cope with the demands of swift, incisive decision-making. Once you have the confidence to trust your own instincts, you're far better geared to cope with adversity and with adverse opinions. No one is suggesting decision-making based on arbitrary, emotional whim, rather, decisions rooted in a sensitivity deeper than conventional intelligence. Leading your-self or your team to victory in the game of life means responding quickly to ever changing situations and events. Responsiveness involves the ability to spot a problem looming, to understand the issues involved and to deal with them swiftly. More important still, in any team situation, leader-responsive-ness posits a flair for understanding the needs, concerns and aspirations of the people around, the knack of melding different people into a single, cohesive unit and the gift of knowing what to delegate most effectively to whom. At work and at home, a good leader needs good interpersonal skills – a concern for the wellbeing of every individual involved.

Belief in People – Team Building

> When business growth and personal growth come together through work, and an organization has a clear common sense of purpose, the results will be awesome.
>
> Mike Bowman – Du Pont Fibres

The simple hierarchies of traditional religious and military leadership models are crumbling. Today's good leader is no longer a remote and auto-cratic figure. The leaders we respond to are like good parents. They recognize the unique value of each person and they work to bring out the best in each individual. Successful families, teams and companies have one major common denominator: they are all groups of individuals who are bonded together by loyalty and supported by a responsive framework. Such group-ings are geared to rise to any challenge placed before them. In today's most effective units, people really do count. Leaders in the game of life succeed by making others feel valued and by actively seeking their involvement – even if this means critical feedback.

> I don't want 'Yes' men around me. I want everyone to tell me the truth, even if it costs them their jobs.
>
> *Sam Goldwyn*

Most people respond favourably to positive feedback, so never forget the importance of *praise*. Clearly communicated and sincerely meant approval is a powerful motivating force. Every potty-training parent knows how well children respond to praise and, in their desire for validation, adults are no different. So praise, praise and praise again. It's amazing how people respond. Your care and concern is crucial in motivating people to get behind you and work with you.

> Most people don't care how much you know until
> they know how much you care.

When you genuinely believe that people, not things, are life's most treasured asset, then you know that compassion can never be an optional extra. Compassion is the cement that binds together the bricks of every relationship. Without care, concern and compassion from the top, there cannot be a contented and truly cohesive unit.

> If you want others to be happy, practise compassion.
> If you want to be happy, practise compassion.
> *Dalai Lama*

The ability to communicate a vision, the openness to ensure that everyone has a genuine opportunity to participate in the decision-making process, the courage to allow opponents to voice their objections, the strength to make decisions and shoulder responsibility, and honesty, frankness and friendship – these are all the qualities of which great team-builders are made. Good leaders know that others will support ideas or plans which they feel they helped to create and in which they had an input. In other words, leaders know and convey that:

> T – TOGETHER
> E – EVERYONE
> A – ACHIEVES
> M – MORE

It has been observed that every goose flying in formation creates an 'uplift' for the birds which follow. By flying in a 'V' formation, the whole flock adds 71 per cent greater flying range than there would be if each bird flew alone. In his award-winning book, *It's Not About the Bike*, cyclist Lance Armstrong relates how he overcame testicular, lung and brain cancer to win that most demanding of physical challenges, the Tour de France, in 1999. He underlines the crucial significance of teamwork by describing how, when cycling on a windy day, his team-mates would stay out in front of him (the team's recognized 'best prospect'), thus shielding him and saving him up to 50 per cent of the work he would otherwise have to have done.

Whatever the area of endeavour, when people elect to work together towards an objective, they will support and encourage one another to reach that objective more swiftly. A good leader encourages the members of the team by maintaining and articulating a clear vision of that final objective.

Passion and Enthusiasm

> Every great and commanding movement in the annals of the
> world is the triumph of enthusiasm. Nothing great was ever
> achieved without it.
>
> Ralph Waldo Emerson

When we love what we're doing, or when we truly believe in what we're
doing, we cannot fail to feel enthusiastic. Enthusiasm is contagious. By
demonstrating your own commitment, passion and enthusiasm, you too
can inspire others to follow in your wake. There's no point demanding
punctuality from your employees if you are constantly late. Equally, there's
no point lecturing your children on the evils of tobacco when you yourself
are on thirty fags a day. To lead, you have to walk the talk. You've got to
show, not tell.

Energy and Positive Demeanour

> Morale drives everything.
>
> Werner Hess

Enthusiasm is closely connected to energy and positive demeanour and it's
difficult to maintain enthusiasm and optimism without sufficient reserves
of energy. To get the best out of yourself, and to maintain the equilibrium
necessary to enable you to encourage and support others around you, it's
vital to ensure 'the healthy mind in the healthy body' which a sensible diet,
regular exercise, and a realistic time-share between family, friends, work

and leisure will help deliver. The way to wellbeing resides in your ability to find and maintain that balance.

Communication Skills

When we consider communication skills, we usually think of people who can convey a message or express themselves well. Increasingly, we are also beginning to realize that communication is not simply one-way traffic. Great communicators not only know how to speak, but also how to listen and, more important still, how to listen *actively*.

Love her or loathe her, Hillary Rodham Clinton is a powerfully persuasive communicator precisely because she employs the technique of active listening. I studied her from close quarters during the 'Vital Voices' conference held in Belfast in spring 1999. Despite the months of scandal and humiliation generated by her husband's well-documented fling with a White House intern, she was clearly 'centred'.

The concept of being 'centred' is as easy to identify as it is difficult to achieve. When great actors appear on stage, they exude a calm confidence which commands attention. In the same way, a good teacher, without even raising her voice, can quell a class of noisy children. Natural history programmes have often shown a similar self-confidence in the 'top' gorilla of any group. While others down the hierarchical scale scuffle and fight for pre-eminence, he strolls regally around his patch, cuffing the odd troublesome youngster, quite clearly the indisputable master of everything he surveys. To be centred is to exude an image of calm, cool and being in control. There is no more powerful a message in the entire lexicon of body language.

Above and beyond the image, however, Hillary Clinton went on to project another very powerful message: the message of *active listening*. For all those present, but especially for the women of Northern Ireland, the importance of knowing that the wife of the (then) President of the United States of America really understood and empathized with their issues cannot be overstated. To achieve centredness, Clinton first *connects* with her audience by thanking individuals personally, by name. She knows, without doubt, that there is nothing more like music to a person's ears than the sound of his or her own name. More effective than this, however, Clinton goes on to recall detailed facts about an individual: that so-and-so has just received an honour, for example, or been appointed to such-and-such a committee.

Cynics may argue that this is simply a result of excellent briefing, but so what? Intelligent leaders understand that people want to believe that their issues have been noted, that their concerns are being attended to and that they themselves are important. In establishing even a few personal connections, communicators like Hillary Clinton manage to relate effectively to their entire audience. Her detailed interest in a few individuals conveys a broader message: that of concern for the group as a whole.

Having established the *connection*, Clinton then goes on to repeat the issues as they have been outlined to her. To a large extent, she simply reiterates what other people have said. To a Northern Ireland audience inured to generations of angry male politicians (alpha plus on shouting, delta minus on listening), this 'mirroring' has a profound effect. People start to believe that for once someone is actually *listening*, rather than simply arguing or haranguing.

Clinton then reinforces the *connection* she has established with her audience by using some well-chosen personal references from her own life (my husband, my daughter, when I was a law student) which demonstrate that she can relate to the people she is addressing. Of course this is a high risk strategy but, as an able politician, Hillary knows how to judge just how much or how little to give away. An audience would soon be alienated by excessive use of this technique but, as a reminder of even the glitziest performer's essential humanity, a few well-chosen personal references serve as very useful anchors.

With apparent effortless simplicity, Hillary Clinton manages to show that she has listened, that she understands and that she cares. In so doing, she makes her audience feel that the vision she then goes on to verbalize is the vision which they themselves have formulated and in which they therefore share. They begin to share her vision and gradually take ownership of it. By showing that she has actively listened, she encourages people to buy into her vision for the future. In addition, her measured voice and the understated determination of her words suggest a capacity to effect change which, in turn, inspires others to act.

Like all good communicators, Clinton knows that when people feel that they count, they automatically feel empowered. In addition, she never ceases to thank or praise, a technique also designed to boost morale. Nothing is more effective in the art of motivation than those two tragically underused expressions of 'Well done!' and 'Thank you!'

On a one-to-one basis, *active listening* involves a few complementary skills. To quote the screen sex goddess, Raquel Welch, 'You can't fake listening. It shows.' For a fruitful dialogue with any individual, remember it's just as important to listen as to speak.

■ Remember, it's just as important to look at people when they're speaking to you as it is when you're speaking to them. Eye contact suggests concern and interest. It invites honesty and candour.
■ Call people by their names.
■ Allow people to finish whatever it is they have to say. Never cut off anyone mid-stream.
■ Try to understand where people are coming from. Remember, it's not

only what they say that's important, but *why* they are saying it, and what has led them to voice such conclusions or sentiments. Try to put yourself in the other person's shoes.

■ Be honest in your reactions and responses. Express genuine feelings. Only honesty can generate effective communication.

■ Don't lay down the law. Even when you're in a position of authority, never impose your view from the outset. Listen carefully to what other people have to say and this will give them the confidence to come up with their own ideas. By encouraging others to speak with honesty, you'll create a shared vision in which everyone has a stake.

> To lead people, it's important to love and listen to them. There is no greater leverage.

CHAPTER THIRTEEN

man of the match

Enthusiasm is the kindling spark which marks the difference between leaders in every activity and the laggards who put in just enough to get by.

Johann Friedrich Schiller

Winners in the game of life are enthusiasts. Enthusiasm is infectious. Enthusiasm engenders enthusiasm. Once we concentrate on the things in life about which we are truly enthusiastic, winning the game of life will follow.

And yet, how many people do you know who exude that vitality which so hallmarks passionate involvement? How many people of your acquaintance are gung-ho enthusiastic about what they are doing or the life they are leading? Take a good look at your fellow travellers on the tube, in the bus, or on the train. Even making allowances for the depressing quality of British public transport, the glum looks on far too many faces suggest lives of quiet desperation. Whenever we read the papers, official statistics on alcohol, drug and nicotine abuse indicate the increasingly high levels of stress and depression in our society. Despite the West's unprecedented material wellbeing, it seems that many people feel unconnected, unhappy and unfulfilled.

Sir Winston Churchill, one of the most inspirational leaders this nation has ever known, once defined success as the ability to move from one failure to another without losing enthusiasm.

And yet everyone, even the great Sir Winston himself, has experienced 'Black Dog' days. We all know those miserable periods when events crowd in and the proverbial light at the end of the tunnel is not even the merest glimmer. Even the rosiest-bespectacled optimist has off-moments, or even entire off-weeks and months, when it is impossible to feel enthusiastic about anything. Life regularly throws up situations such as death, divorce and dismissal, where grief and depression are the normal, 'healthy' reactions, and to which the only remedy is the great healer of time.

But what happens when despondency is not merely the normal reaction to a specific, unfortunate event? What happens when a sense of being stuck in a rut of despondency starts to become a way of life? In cases of severe, so-called endogenous depression, professional help is advisable. Thankfully, however, not everyone finds themselves completely paralysed by such a critical condition. Far more prevalent are the instances of folk who simply feel tired, washed-out and lacking in *enthusiasm*. The statistics on alcohol, drugs and anti-depressants suggest that far too many people are not 'happy in their skin'. These quick-fix solutions, however, are merely short-term palliatives and are of no help in addressing the fundamental issues of our general wellbeing.

Hundreds of thousands – perhaps even millions – of people are functioning at a fraction of their full capacity. These are the people who settle for just existing; the people who have given up on getting passionately involved in the game of life. These are the people who perform adequately, or even highly effectively, in certain areas of their lives. But if they're not feeling the *joy* and *vitality* that so hallmark enthusiasts, then they're not living but simply surviving. You can't be a winner if you're not even a player. Without enthusiasm, you're relegated to the sidelines of the real game of life.

People who love life find it easy to be enthusiastic. These are the optimists who win where the pessimists fail. Of course, pessimists may win in spite of themselves, but optimists will always achieve results more easily. Optimists are not simplistic Pollyannas but rather realists who think positively, or activists who know how to channel their enthusiasm into achieving the results they want. A positive mind-set, together with the energy to fight for an objective, forms the basis of the enthusiasm which marks out winners.

Time and time again we see that the real difference between optimists and pessimists rarely lies in ability, but in a state of mind. However, apart from mind-set, there is also a question of stamina and staying power. Whatever the odds, optimists refuse to give up. They just keep on trying and, because they persevere, they are successful in the end. Pessimists, on the contrary, lose heart and give up.

According to business and sporting entrepreneur Nigel Wray: 'Too many people allow themselves to fall very cosily into the "Can't do" category. It's all important, if you want to succeed, to be a "Can do" person.'

Optimism is never the easy option. Optimism demands courage, effort and pain because it involves accepting the challenge that the pessimist refuses. In picking up the gauntlet, the optimist is probably defying the odds and his behaviour may even seem irrational to the vast majority of timid souls.

George Bernard Shaw once noted that the irrational man seeks to adapt the world to himself, whereas the rational man seeks to adapt himself to the world. 'Therefore,' he concluded wryly, 'all progress is made by irrational men.'

Throughout history, conventional wisdom has insisted that all manner of things were impossible. 'A flying machine? Impossible!' 'Land a man on the moon? Impossible!' 'A sub-four minute mile? Never!' And yet all these, and billions more, 'impossible' feats have been accomplished by 'irrational' individuals who refused to accept the word 'can't' in their personal lexicon. Their optimism succeeded in moulding the world to suit their version of events. The force of their enthusiasm prevailed.

> Nothing great was ever achieved without enthusiasm.
>
> *Ralph Waldo Emerson (1803–82)*

There is, however, a role for the pessimist which is a perfectly valid one. Both internally, within ourselves, and externally, in our families, communities or organizations. 'You've got to have "Doctor Death" round, says Sir Martin Sorrell, 'and before you make a major decision you must listen to his views on the possible downside. Then it's up to you to work out the pluses and the minuses. But you've got to have the guts to take the final decision and, in making that decision, you've got to be positive.'

Optimists are usually winners because they *make* things happen. Pessimists are often losers because they *let* things happen. According to Archie Norman, 'Optimists lead; Pessimists advise. And yes, admittedly, the pessimists are the ones who occasionally have to mop up afterwards!'

The crucial characteristic of the winners in life is that they are not only optimistic and enthusiastic when things are going well, but equally so when things are going badly. Winners in the game of life treat the twin imposters of triumph and disaster with the same degree of pragmatism and understanding. They realize that success may harbour its own seeds of destruction if arrogance and complacency are allowed to set in. The many people who have given so generously of their time in the compilation of this book have all had their fair share of success and adversity. The following coping strategies are drawn from their personal experience.

SURVIVAL TECHNIQUES IN TRIUMPH

1. Share success with others and talk about it. Build on it and reward people according to their merits.
2. Manage success with modesty. Never become arrogant or complacent or you'll get tripped up very quickly. Remember, there's always something new to achieve.
3. Try constantly to improve on current standards.
4. Continue to build on your success and acknowledge that future success may be harder, and take longer, to achieve.
5. Remember that only your personal life is 'real'. The concept of 'success' is largely irrelevant, so don't get carried away by it.
6. Remember that you're only as good as your last project.
7. Keep your equilibrium. Keep your feet firmly on the ground. Don't let your ego grow. Enjoy success, but never believe it will last for ever.
8. Recognize achievement. Make time to mark your success and reward the troops. Have some fun and enjoy yourself, but work hard too – continually review objectives and set new goals.

9. In success, combine a firm grasp of reality with a sense of humour. In adversity, do the same.

10. Never trust approaches made after good publicity. Remain yourself, do not become your new image.

11. In success, be aware of the dual danger signs of excitement and complacency.

12. Keep in touch with all your networks, especially your home and your family.

13. Praise success quietly but sincerely. Ensure it does not go to your own or to anyone else's head, although there's no harm in publicizing your success if it helps you get what you want.

14. Keep a keen sense of the ridiculous and a keen awareness of human frailty.

15. In success, you must maintain momentum, keep people focussed, and enable them to learn from what they do well.

16. Share success. Accept blame for failure.

SURVIVAL TECHNIQUES IN ADVERSITY

1. Reflect on what is happening and why. Break the problem down into bite-sized chunks and work out what you can change.

2. Keep adversity in proportion. Seek to limit its effects and set clear, achievable priorities for addressing it.

3. Remain focussed on your goals and look for different ways of achieving them. Tough it out and believe that you will win in the end.

4. Whatever happens, keep faith in yourself.

5. Success means winning more often than losing. Adversity must be seen

as a part of life. When things are going wrong, remember that adversity teaches lessons and strengthens character. Adversity accelerates learning.

6. When things go wrong, feel free to get depressed! Then, either cut your losses or try and put things right. At the same time, keep things in perspective. Concentrate on the positives in your life – for example health, family and friendship.

7. You've got to work through adversity. Develop action plans so that you feel in control and that you're doing something about the problem.

8. Look for ways to motivate yourself or your team. Look for quick wins, however small, to create confidence.

9. Be honest with yourself and other people and always listen to and recognize bad news.

10. Keep a low profile and take the blame.

11. Don't take it personally.

12. Work even harder and keep even busier. Show doggedness and attempt to hold on to memories of better times.

13. Keep a sense of proportion. Identify the things that are worrying you and ring-fence them in your mind. In other words, put adversity in a mental box and sit on it. This ensures that problems in one area of your life do not spill over into all the others. Then get on with enjoying life as best you can.

14. Show determination and try and dream up the *bright idea* which will cut through that apparently intractable problem.

15. Grit your teeth and remember your long-term goals as long as a realistic reassessment confirms their validity.

16. As with success, so with adversity. Understand the transitory nature of both.

17. In the case of adversity, make sure you have other compensating interests to divert you.
18. Realize it could be worse.

Feeling down has many causes, and often there is no easy remedy. If, for no obvious physical reasons, you're feeling weary, if you've lost (or can't even remember) that *joie de vivre* that makes life worthwhile, then it's time to stop contemplating the symptoms and to start attacking the sources.

ARE YOU SUFFERING FROM 'ENTHUSIASM DEFICIENCY' SYNDROME?

Do you recognize any of the following symptoms?

- When you contemplate your life, do you feel unhappy, depressed or unable to relax?
- Do you have difficulty believing that life can ever be a joy for you?
- Do you feel that, however hard you work, you seem to be making no progress, that you are merely existing rather than living?
- Do you ever wonder what it is, niggling away inside you, that seems to be sapping your energy and stifling your enthusiasm for life?

Most people, even those who appear to lead glittering, successful lives, will at some point suffer from some or all of these symptoms. Why else do so many apparently rich, beautiful and successful people end up in the Betty Ford Clinic?

People who are suffering from Enthusiasm Deficiency Syndrome are usually suffering from a lack of *balance* in their lives. Losing balance does not happen overnight. It creeps up on you so stealthily, you're not even aware it's happening. It may be the work commitments that result in your child's birthday party being missed; or the dress that you bought with your credit card, that you know you can't afford; or maybe even the occasional over-indulgence in the wine bar. Without careful monitoring, however, the 'occasional' has a nasty habit of becoming the norm. Your all-important balance is lost and, with that, your fundamental mental, physical and emotional wellbeing.

To the outside world, you may even be considered successful, especially if your loss of balance is due to an obsession for work. But whatever the reason, a loss of balance still results in a loss of perspective, which in turn means a disturbance in your all-important physical, mental and spiritual balance. Herein lie the roots of Enthusiasm Deficiency Syndrome.

BACK TO BASICS – WHERE HAS THE 'VOOMPH!' GONE?

Why are some people full of zest for life while others are stuck in a rut? Since nothing – neither money, position, power nor status – can guarantee the voomph of enthusiasm, there clearly are no simple answers. In less enlightened days, the somewhat unsympathetic advice for any lack of voomph was to pull your socks up and snap out of it. Nowadays, a goodly proportion of the nation prefers Prozac to sock pulling, but the underlying problem remains the same. If you don't identify the reasons *why* you're feeling low, negative and lacking in voomph, how will you ever be able to deal with them? In the short term, Prozac and sock pulling may have their place. But without a clear understanding of the root problem, the symptoms are likely to persist.

WHAT'S HOLDING YOU BACK?

There is a school of thought which maintains that you can learn to control your emotions. Once you've learned to control your emotions, you can feel anything you want to feel, whatever happens, and for no reason – simply because you *want* to feel it. No one can control events, but if you can control how you *react* to those events, then you're truly in control of your life. How can you control your emotions if you don't first understand how those feelings have come about? In order to confront your demons, you first have to know what those demons look like, where they came from and why they have such a hold on you.

For years, even into adulthood, I was petrified of the dark. Admittedly, many people are frightened of darkness: fear of the night and of the unknown terrors that may be lurking in the dark is an atavistic fear passed down from generation to generation over the millennia. But my fear had reached such proportions that I couldn't sleep at night without all the lights in the house left blazing. When the electricity bill reached Blackpool Illuminations proportions, I resolved to discover *why*.

The process took some time, but eventually I managed to pinpoint the exact place and time that the fear took root. As a small child, someone had given me a luminous statue which was guaranteed to glow in the dark. I decided to test out its glow-factor in the darkest place I could think of: the back of my mother's wardrobe. As I stepped inside the closet, the door clicked shut. There I was – a tiny, petrified child – and suddenly the clothes seemed intent on wrapping themselves around my face and trying to smother me. It was pitch dark. I banged hysterically on the door, but no one heard me for what seemed to me like a *very* long time. I felt terrified and helpless.

This was an example of a simple childhood prank that misfired. Viewed objectively, it would not seem seriously traumatic and yet its effects on me were long-term and disturbing. The point is that, in life, it is not *what* happens to you that matters. It's *how you perceive* what happens to you that really matters. In my particular case, the plain facts are that I remained locked in a wardrobe for no more than two minutes before my mother heard and released me. But when you're only five years old, very small, and locked in a dark, claustrophobic wardrobe, two minutes seem like an eternity.

I have deliberately chosen a completely trivial incident and described the detrimental effects which ensued. In cases where a person has been seriously and actively abused, the psychological scarring may be intense. Since it is not what happens to you, but how you perceive what happens to you that matters, harm may be caused by actions which are not even obviously or deliberately harmful.

Take the example of a woman I know who was brought up in a male-dominated household which was warm, loving and kind but where the only conversation over the dinner table was sport. Every time she opened her mouth to express an opinion on the only subject that was ever discussed, her elder brothers simply talked straight across her, a constant act of bad behaviour that went unchecked by her parents. She soon began to feel that no one ever wanted to hear anything that she, a girl, had to say and eventually she gave up even trying to express opinions, not only on sport but on any other subject. It is hardly surprising that later on in life, this woman fell into a number of unhappy relationships with domineering men who ignored her unexpressed feelings and trampled all over her. A beautiful, smart, clever, eminently capable but unassertive woman, she became increasingly withdrawn and depressed. Certainly, she demonstrated no signs of the 'voomph' life she could and should have been living.

There had been no overt cruelty in her life. On the contrary, as a child, she had been cossetted: the best schools, wonderful holidays, a country house and her own pony. But the fact that in *her* mind she was a person of little value, whose views were not worth hearing, created within her a powerful, negative self-image which she carried into adulthood.

I'm pleased to say that the timorous woman I first met ten years ago is now a highly successful businesswoman. She grew so tired of her joyless, passive existence and her shut-up-and-listen-to-me relationships that she decided to go back to basics, confront her demons, and expel her negative self-image. Reading the paper recently, I was delighted to see that one City analyst (male, need one add) had even labelled her 'stroppy'.

Getting back to basics is not about wallowing in self-pity or crying over spilt milk. Getting back to basics is about understanding why you feel the way you feel and why you react the way you react. Only when you understand your reactions and emotions can you start to control them. Only then can you achieve the balance and equanimity required to cope with life's inevitable ups and downs. Only then can you start to enjoy playing the game of life.

REVIVE THE VOOMPH. ASK YOURSELF WHEN AND WHY

Take time to understand the habits, patterns and knee-jerk emotional reactions which are keeping you stuck in those same self-destructive cycles. If for years you've been feeding yourself a diet of negative messages (I don't count; I'm only loveable if I'm slim/beautiful/rich; everyone is out to get me; I can't make it on my own etc.), then negative thinking has become a habit so deeply rooted in your subconscious that you're probably not even aware of it. The time frame involved may not even be years. A few knocks, a bad relationship, a job lost, a contract blown and negative thinking can swiftly set in. Negative thinking is like a malignant tumour which, if left unchecked, will soon invade and destroy everything around it.

Successful people maintain a positive mental attitude because they constantly feed themselves positive messages (I am good enough; I'm love-able as I am; I can do anything I put my mind to; I am bound to win this race/match/contract etc.). A positive mind-set is all-important in both enjoying and winning the game of your life. How often have you met two people of similar education, background and ability whose lives have taken dramatically different paths because of their differences in outlook? When you're feeling down, the challenge is to turn a negative self-image into a positive self-definition. To achieve this, you must go back and pinpoint when the negative, disempowering, enthusiasm-sapping messages began.

The point of this exercise is not to go back in time to stay. This is not an invitation to apportion blame or to parent-bash, but rather to understand your current feelings. It is an opportunity to confront and understand past events that are still affecting you negatively. Only when you have revisited these situations can you junk the rubbish that's dragging you down and move on.

Focus

Try to go back to a specific event where you actually experienced whatever it is that you now want insight into. One highly successful entrepreneur I interviewed told me that he used to find it very hard to function effectively because he could never trust anyone. When he realized this about himself, he tried to establish the reasons why by looking back into the events of his past. When he thought about it, he began to recall a very hurtful example of being let down by his best friend at school. The message he had internalized as a small boy was, therefore, to trust no one. His lack of trust resulted in a reluctance to communicate with anyone and, hardly surprisingly, he found that people reacted by being wary, suspicious and, ultimately, unresponsive and unreliable. The vicious circle was thus reinforced. When he decided to go back to the root of his mistrust (an event which took place forty years previously), he began to understand it for what it was: an isolated incident of betrayal. It was at this point that he managed to break a destructive habit which, for him, had become a way of life.

Write Yourself a Positive Script

The man in question had made a classic, enthusiasm-sapping mistake. He made a general assumption on the basis of one individual example. He had unwittingly allowed one particular incident of betrayal to inform his entire outlook and modus operandi. 'My mate's a rotter', became 'Everyone under the sun is a rotter.' The key to winning the game of life is never to generalize unless you're talking about Millwall fans. Don't tell yourself you're thick, just because you struggle with Maths. Don't go thinking you're a loser just because you failed to clinch the deal. Never allow the particular to become the general. Ring-fence your failures, faults and mistakes. Don't allow them to spoil the rest of your life.

Box-up the Botch-up!

So what if you bought the wrong jam and the children all threw wobblies? Whatever the commercials may suggest to the contrary, that doesn't make you a lousy mother! We're all constantly making mistakes and experiencing failures but we mustn't allow those glitches to affect our entire lives. The moment you allow negative feelings in one area of your life to spill over into others, you'll constantly feel down and disheartened.

In the game of life, winners never jump to conclusions. They know that there are few things more destructive in life than beating yourself up with conclusions unsupported by facts. So don't go telling yourself you're completely useless just because you didn't get the job. Who knows? It could be that the bloke who landed the position ahead of you is the chairman's nitwit nephew. Never fall prey to irrational conclusions and, whatever happens, try to keep that all-important sense of perspective.

Where Am I Blocked?

Ask yourself where you're feeling blocked. Is this debilitating sensation due to:

1. lack of opportunity
2. lack of self-motivation
3. lack of practice
4. lack of self-confidence?

Lack of Opportunity

If you keep on doing the same old things, you'll keep on getting the same old results. If you feel that your life or your business is not thriving, get out and about more, move into more circles and increase the odds of coming across the right person/job/solution/lifestyle.

Lack of Self-motivation

If you're not feeling motivated, the chances are that you don't want to do what you find yourself doing. Take time to reflect on what you really want to do. Once your objective is clear, make the necessary changes to enable you to go ahead and do it.

Lack of Practise

This is entirely within your control. The greatest mistake you can ever make is being afraid to make one. Keep at it! It may be a good old golfing cliché, but the fact remains that the more you practise, the luckier you get. Luck is what happens to you when you keep on trying.

Lack of Self-confidence

As we've seen, confidence will grow once the roots of the debilitating self-doubt have been identified and destroyed. Practice, rehearsal, repetition, exposure, extending your own boundaries, moving outside your own comfort zone, creating a positive self-image and scripting positive messages for yourself – these are all 'confidence-building measures'. As Voltaire once observed, 'No problem can sustain the assault of sustained thinking.'

> Whenever you feel like throwing in the towel in the game of life, take time out to *think* your way through it.
> Mull your way to Man of the Match.

CHAPTER FOURTEEN

the final whistle

There will be times when everything appears to be going swimmingly and you feel you're winning the game of your life. Now is the time to beware. Coping with winning is much more difficult than it sounds. Once you've achieved some degree of success, it's very tempting to sit back on your laurels and, before you know it, the dreaded rot of complacency has set in. Complacency is the greatest threat to any successful individual, team or company and the swiftest road to failure. You've got to keep moving forward by setting new goals and creating new challenges.

> Remember, success is a journey, not a destination
> and you've never, ever finished.

However well you feel you're doing, manage your success with modesty. The moment you become arrogant or complacent, there'll be plenty of people only too happy to trip you up. By showing consideration for people less lucky and privileged than you, you'll keep your feet planted firmly on the ground.

'Whoever you are and whatever you've achieved,' says Sir Victor Blank, 'never start thinking you're better than the waiter or the cab driver.'

Winners in the game of life maintain a sense of proportion both in triumph and disaster. Whatever life throws at them, they continue to demonstrate the crucial human attributes of understanding, generosity and good manners.

Real winners in the game of life have a burning desire to help others be winners also. As parents, we try our utmost to nurture our children through infancy, childhood, puberty and adolescence, and we hope to see them safely on their way to responsible, autonomous adulthood. As individuals, we try to help our family and friends whenever they need our support. And as leaders in a family, team or community, we endeavour to direct and encourage those for whom we are responsible.

To be a winner in the game of life, establish a *clear vision* of who you are and who you want to be. Decide on your own destination.

Work out how to make this vision a reality. *Plan* which route you intend to take in order to arrive at your desired destination.

Learn how to sell yourself and, along with yourself, the vision and plan you wish to promote. *Communicate* your ideas effectively by painting clear pictures for others. Show *patience* when *listening* to other people's views and concerns, and develop the *wisdom* to accept any constructive input people have to offer.

Be *flexible* in your approach and prepared to adapt your game plan to accommodate the demands of an ever evolving situation.

Never be afraid to show your *enthusiasm*. Enthusiasm is infectious. When you're *passionate* about your project, you'll soon convince others to join in.

Keep your eye on the *big picture* but *pay attention to detail*. When the game of your life just isn't going according to plan, fine tune wherever it's appropriate.

Have the *courage* to *aspire*, to *risk* and to *achieve*. Muster the guts to admit mistakes, to learn the lessons and to move on.

Be *versatile* and take up the challenge of *lifelong learning*. Be prepared to acquire new skills and grasp new, exciting opportunities.

> Whatever happens, you'll be a winner in the game of life if you simply keep on trying.

It is not the critic who counts, nor the man who points out how the strong man stumbles or where the doer of deeds could have done better. The credit belongs to the man who is actually in the arena, whose face is marred by dust and sweat and blood and who knows great enthusiasm, great devotion and the triumph of achievement, and who, if he fails, at least fails while daring greatly, so that his place will never be with those odd and timid souls who know neither victory or defeat. You've never lived until you've almost died. For those who have had to fight for it, life has truly a flavour the protected shall never know.

Theodore Roosevelt

> So long as you're out there, giving your best, you're winning the game of life.

index

ability   5, 28, 69, 72, 116, 124,
        147
acceptance   2
achievement   3, 5, 31, 33, 105
    achievable goals   13–14
adversity   58, 62–3, 107
    coping strategies   150–2
    dealing with   54–6
    and decision-making   136
    leadership and   125, 128
advice   35, 125, 127
Alexander the Great   113
anger   44–5

anxiety   3, 46–7
Aristotle   65
Armstrong, Lance: *It's Not About
        the Bike*   139
Astronaut Syndrome   66–7
Atherton, Michael   15, 49, 101,
        125–6
athletes   82, 98–9

balance   4, 5–6, 62, 127, 141
    emotional   49
    loss of   153
Barker, Joel   131

Beckham, David   14
beliefs   26, 57, 68, 93–5, 100–1, 128
    and feelings   107–8
    and motivation   86
    negative   93, 104–6
    positive   93, 102–3
    and slippage   108–9
    see also self-belief
Bird, Larry   65
Bismarck, Otto von   35
Blank, Sir Victor   xiii, 94, 120, 134,
    162
Body Shop   57
Bowman, Mike   137
Branson, Sir Richard   xiv
Brearley, Mike: *The Art of
    Captaincy*   125
Brown, Charlie   135
Bryant, Bear   25
buddies   61
business   18, 57, 62, 114–17, 134

Carphone Warehouse   119
Carroll, Lewis: *Alice in Wonderland*
    121–2
centredness   130, 141–2
change   17–23, 30, 32, 34, 63, 102
charisma   113, 118
Churchill, Sir Winston   105, 146

Circle Theory   40
clarity   8–9, 12, 118, 119, 128
Clinton, Hillary Rodham   141–3
Cockerell, Michael   102
common sense   111, 114, 127
communication   73, 106, 158, 162
    electronic   117
    and leadership   113, 115, 118,
        122, 123, 128, 141–4
    with stakeholders   54–6, 59–60
community   5, 68
compartmentalization   44–51
compassion   113, 118, 121, 138,
    143
    fatigue   76
competition   96, 103
complacency   66, 149, 161
compromise   13, 33, 34–5, 58
conclusions, jumping to   159
confidence   21, 38, 102, 122
    and form   87
    and leadership   126, 130, 136,
        141
    lack of   87–8, 101, 160
    as motivation   86
    negative influences   27
    pretended   100
    reinforcement of   96–8, 106,
        151

consistency 66

control 5, 13, 105, 151
   emotional 107, 154
   and fitness 48
   and leadership 121

convictions, *see* beliefs

coping strategies 45–6, 56, 149–52

courage 2, 71, 73, 163
   in adversity 41, 49, 108
   and leadership 112–13, 119, 125, 127, 133–5
   and optimism 147
   and principles 57, 58, 94–5

creativity 27, 90, 125, 129, 131–2

customer service 116–17, 119–20

Dalai Lama 138

Darwin, Charles 17

decision-making 148
   courage in 133–5
   and leadership 119, 120, 135–6, 138

defeat 71–2

deferred gratification 83

delegation 77, 120, 123, 128, 137

depression 42, 48–9, 97, 146, 151, 152

and decision-making 134
and negative beliefs 104
and time management 76

determination 2, 69, 71, 120, 126, 151

development 26, 32

disability 18, 72, 81

disappointment 44, 56

discipline 50–1, 63, 82–3, 90, 120, 136

disempowerment 104–6, 157

dreams 7–8, 33, 113, 131

dumpers/dumpees 76–9

Dunstone, Chris 119

Edison, Thomas Alva 75

Edmonds, Frances 17

Edmonds, Phil xiv

education 19, 103

efficiency 126

Eisenhower, Dwight D. 115

Emerson, Ralph Waldo 140, 148

emotion 120, 136
   control of 107, 154
   emotional balance 49
   emotional intelligence 113
   emotional upheaval 108–9
   understanding basis of 154–7

empathy   113, 115, 118, 125, 127,
    142–3
empowerment   101–3, 122–3,
    143
encouragement   84–6, 106, 119,
    124, 139
energy   xv, 69, 73, 81, 105, 108, 147
    deficiency   70–1
    and leadership   113, 127, 140–1
    sapping of   45
enthusiasm   xv, 49, 86, 103, 106,
    145–9, 163
    Deficiency Syndrome   152–3
    and leadership   125, 126, 127,
        130, 140
    pseudo-enthusiasm   84
ethics   15, 26, 94, 103, 127, 128
Euripides   7
excellence   65–9
exercise   48, 140
experience   27, 38, 105
exploitative dumpitis   78

failure   125
    and confidence   87
    coping with   49–51
    learning from   11–12, 41–2
    negativity arising from   44–9
    and planning   20, 63

ring-fencing   43–4, 97, 158–9
    thoughts of   99
Faldo, Nick   66
family   4, 26, 68, 70, 96, 162
    exploitative dumpitis in   78–9
    leadership   117–18, 122–3, 136
    as stakeholders   53–4
Fangio, Juan Mañuel   66
fear   22–3, 38, 70, 100, 133, 154
feedback   137–8
fine tuning   163
fitness   34, 48
flexibility   58–60, 90, 116, 162
focus   61, 69, 150, 157–8
    and leadership   119–20, 127,
        136
Fonteyn, Dame Margot   88
form   87
friends   5, 26, 31, 68, 96, 139, 162
Frost, Sir David   xiii
frustration   3, 8, 29, 30, 45–6, 76,
        78
fun   5, 31, 50, 88–90, 149

game of life:
    rules of   2–4
    WellBeing Plan   xv
game plan   20, 23, 25–36, 38,
        62–3

Gandhi, Mahatma   95, 130
Gavaskar, Sunil   xiv
generalizations   43, 97, 158
generosity   2, 119, 127, 162
goals   xv, 7–16, 25, 63, 66, 128, 134
Goldwyn, Sam   137
Graham, Billy   133
Gretzky, Wayne   11

Hadlee, Sir Richard   xiv
Hamlet (Shakespeare) 130
happiness   32, 107
hard work   13, 27, 71, 75, 131, 149,
    151
Heine, Heinrich   93
Hesburgh, Father T.   129
Hess, Werner   140
Heyhoe-Flint, Rachael   126
hierarchy   115, 116, 137
Hill, Napoleon   131
Hillary, Sir Edmund   67
honesty   2, 151
    belief in   27, 102, 108
    and communication   143,
        144
    and leadership   125, 130, 132,
        138
Horses for Courses theory   114,
    118–28

Houghton, James R.   116
housewives   28

imagination   33, 84–5, 129, 130–1
influences, negative   27
information   38, 136
    technology   115–17
integrity   2, 5, 27, 102, 108
    and leadership   125, 127, 129,
        132, 135
intelligence   119, 127, 128
intuition   136
involvement   85, 101
ISSIMO lists   4

Jerome, Jerome K.   90
job loss   18, 43, 55, 107–8
joy   2, 147, 152
judgement   120
justice   124

Keller, Helen   90
Khan, Imran   xiv
King, Martin Luther   95, 131
Kipling, Rudyard   49

Lao-Tzu   111–12
leadership   xv, 102, 111–28
    qualities   129–44

learning   45, 86, 123–4
    lifelong   xv, 163
    from mistakes   11–12, 41–2,
        151
LeBoeuf, Dr Michael   135
leisure   26, 89, 105
lifestyle   33–4, 60–1, 69, 70–1
Lillee, Dennis   xiv
Lincoln, Abraham   107
Lippman, Walter   111
listening   113, 121, 125, 128,
        141–4, 162
Lloyd, David   101
loyalty   115, 137
luck   39–40, 127

McLuhan, Marshall   117
Manchester United   39
Mandela, Nelson   42, 95, 120, 131
Matthews, Bernard   69
memories   87–8, 151
mentor   35, 118
meritocracy   115
midlife crisis   70
mistakes   11–12, 41–3, 105, 158–9,
        163
modesty   149, 162
money   5, 31, 86
Morgan, Cliff   37, 119

motivation   83–4, 102, 151
    of others   5, 84–6, 113, 125,
        127, 138, 143
    self-motivation   19, 31, 39, 50,
        80, 160

Napoleon   134
negativity   13, 71, 95, 156–7
    disempowering beliefs   104–6
    ring-fencing   43–4, 97, 159
    and worry   46
Nelson, Dr Liz   69
Nightingale, Earl   7
Nin, Anaïs   70
Norman, Archie   127, 148

obstacles   33, 42, 71–2, 100, 106
opinions   94
opportunity   40, 81, 89, 90, 108,
        159, 163
optimism   94, 102, 104, 126, 140,
        147–9
O'Rourke, P.J.   70
other people   4, 14, 22, 26, 106
    belief in   130, 137–9
    motivating   5, 84–6, 113
    see also stakeholders
overachievement   5, 27
over-direction   123

overload   76
over-scheduling   90

Parkinson, Michael   5, 15, 102
passion   10, 31, 71, 84–5, 147, 163
    and leadership   120, 130, 140
Pasteur, Louis   127
patience   51, 162
people skills   120, 137
perception   154
perseverance   49–51, 57, 68, 101,
        106, 120, 147
personal relationships   6, 26
personality   28–9
perspective   159
pessimism   46, 94, 147–8
physical challenge   26–7
physical wellbeing   108
planning   9, 12, 16, 37–8, 162
    managing change   18, 20–1
    proactive   21–3
    see also game plan
positive mindset   13, 18, 38–9,
        70–1, 157, 160
    in adversity   108
    empowering beliefs   93, 101–3
    and enthusiasm   147
    and leadership   130, 140–1
    visualization   51, 98–100

    and worry   47
positive reinforcement   95–7
power   123
practice   160
praise   138, 143, 150
principles   57–8, 86, 132
priorities   15, 80
proactivity   13, 19, 21–3, 46
problems   71–3, 81, 96, 97, 99–100,
        150
proportion, sense of   162

reality   8, 13, 33, 150
Reeve, Christopher   81
relevance   14–15
relaxation   5, 26
respect   113, 123, 125, 126
responsibility   119, 130, 135–7, 138
responsiveness   130, 135–7
Rice, Sir Tim   5, 15, 102
Roddick, Anita   57, 132
Roosevelt, Theodore   163
Ross, David   119–20

sacrifice   13, 60, 62, 94, 131
satisfaction   4, 15, 30–1
Schiller, Johann Friedrich   145
self, sense of   129, 130–1
self-assertiveness   79

self-belief   xv, 2, 38, 71–2, 87, 95–8,
      100, 130
self-confidence, *see* confidence
self-congratulation   2, 90–1
self-esteem   130
self-image   156
self-improvement   2
self-knowledge   41, 69, 129, 130–1
self-mastery   107
self-reliers   77
setbacks, *see* failure
Shaw, George Bernard   148
short-termism   11, 12, 14
simplicity   10–11, 12–13, 40
skills   18, 26, 28, 34, 45, 163
slippage   108
Smith, Delia   39
Sorrell, Sir Martin   xiv, 40, 50, 71,
      93, 133, 148
spontaneity   16, 40
sport   66–7, 82, 87, 98, 101, 119
stakeholders   34, 51, 53–7, 59–60
standards, self-imposed   67–9
step-by-step approach   11
stress   3, 20, 70, 76, 78, 80, 114,
      134, 146
success   39, 91, 102
   coping with   149–50, 161–2
   defining   4–6

rehearsing   66
and satisfaction   30
strategies   98–100
support   34, 35–6, 47, 54–7, 60, 86,
      118, 139
   networks   36, 50, 61–2
survival techniques   149–52

talent   66, 102, 115, 116, 119,
      124
'TATT' syndrome   70
teachers   123–4, 141
teamwork   115, 116, 118, 122, 130,
      137–9
temperament   28–9
Teresa, Mother   95, 130, 132
Thatcher, Margaret   81
Thompson, Daley   98
time-barring   16, 47
time management   76, 89
tough love   121
Tracy, Brian   9
training   13, 114
trust   86, 100, 123, 130, 157–8
Tyson, Mike   95

understanding   2, 113, 125, 127,
      136, 162
   self-understanding   154–8

values   4, 14, 15, 26, 80–1, 132
verification, external   106
versatility   163
vision   15, 42, 85–6, 103, 143, 144,
        162
    of leader   112, 119–21, 123, 127,
        129, 131–2, 136
visualization   98–100
Voltaire   160

walking the talk   124
Warne, Shane   xiv
Waterstone, Tim   128
Welch, John F. Jr   117

Welch, Raquel   143
WellBeing cricket match
        xiii–xiv
WellBeing Plan   xv
Wingfield Digby, Revd Andrew
        101
wisdom   42, 162
work   xv, 5, 35–6, 45, 68, 70, 78,
        88–9
    effectiveness   75–91
    leadership   122–3
    see also business
worry   20, 46–8, 70, 73, 100, 105
Wray, Nigel   xiv, 100–1, 120, 147